HEROIC MOCKERY

Chas. Addams's cartoon of a self-assured but minuscule Minotaur awaiting the arrival of experimental rats at the center of a laboratory maze suggests the jocoserious ways in which Joyce employs the myth of the labyrinth of Daedalus throughout *Ulysses* and, especially, at the center of the book. Since Joyce, following Homer, Virgil, Ovid, and Pope, exploited the rich heroic and mock-heroic potentials of this ancient myth, as explained in chapter 4, the cartoon provides a succinct illustration of the culminating motif of *Heroic Mockery*. (Drawing by Chas. Addams; © 1976 The New Yorker Magazine, Inc.)

HEROIC MOCKERY

Variations on Epic Themes from Homer to Joyce

George deForest Lord

NEWARK
UNIVERSITY OF DELAWARE PRESS
London: Associated University Presses

©1977 by Associated University Presses, Inc.

Associated University Presses, Inc.
Cranbury, New Jersey 08512

Associated University Presses
Magdalen House
136-148 Tooley Street
London SE1 2TT, England

Library of Congress Cataloging in Publication Data

Lord, George de Forest, 1919-
    Heroic mockery.

    Bibliography: p.
    Includes index.
2. Literature, Comparative—English and classical.
3. Literature, Comparative—Classical and English.
I. Title.
PN6149.M55L6   809   76-13930
ISBN 0-87413-117-0

I wish to thank the following publishers for having given me permission to quote from copyrighted material:

Doubleday & Company, Inc., for permission to quote from Homer, THE ILIAD, translated by Robert Fitzgerald, Copyright © 1974 by Robert Fitzgerald, Reprinted by permission of Doubleday & Company, Inc.; and from Homer. THE ODYSSEY, translated by Robert Fitzgerald, Copyright © 1961 by Robert Fitzgerald. Reprinted by permission of Doubleday & Company, Inc.

Little, Brown and Company, for permission to quote from DECLINE AND FALL by Evelyn Waugh, by permission of Little, Brown and Co. Copyright 1928, 1929, © 1956 by Evelyn Waugh.

The New American Library, Inc., for quotations reprinted from ANTONY AND CLEOPATRA by William Shakespeare, edited by Barbara Everett. Copyright © 1964 by Barbara Everett. By arrangement with The New American Library, Inc., New York, New York. And for quotations reprinted from THE HISTORY OF HENRY IV, Part One, by William Shakespeare, edited by Maynard Mack. Copyright © 1965 by Maynard Mack. Copyright © 1963 by Sylvan Barnet. By arrangement with The New American Library, Inc., New York, New York.

The Viking Press, Inc., for permission to quote from OVID: THE METAMORPHOSES translated by Horace Gregory. Copyright © 1958 by The Viking Press, Inc. Reprinted by permission of The Viking Press.

PRINTED IN THE UNITED STATES OF AMERICA

For P. M., Jr.

"Having therefore resolved to be a doing, and deeming that time improper for any serious concerns, I thought good to divert myself with drawing up a panegyrick upon Folly. How! what maggot (say you) put this in your head? Why the first hint, Sir, was your own surname of More, which comes as near the literal sound of the word [Moria — Folly] as you yourself are distant from the signification of it. . . ."

—Erasmus, *The Praise of Folly*

Mock mockers after that
That would not lift a hand maybe
To help good, wise or great
To bar that foul storm out, for we
Traffic in mockery.

— Yeats, "Nineteen Hundred and Nineteen"

As we have learned from Huizinga and more recent writers like Josef Pieper and Harvey Cox, the only secure truth men have is that which they themselves create and dramatize; to live is to play at the meaning of life. The upshot of this whole tradition of thought is that it teaches us once and for all that childlike foolishness is the calling of mature men.

— Ernest Becker, *The Denial of Death*

Contents

Other books by *George deForest Lord:*

Homeric Renaissance: the "Odyssey" of George Chapman
Poems on Affairs of State: Augustan Satirical Verse, 1660-1714
 Volume 1
Andrew Marvell, Complete Poetry
Andrew Marvell, A Collection of Critical Essays
Anthology of Poems on Affairs of State

Acknowledgments

Rarely has a book so small incurred such a heavy load of indebtedness. To mention only contemporary writers on play and game theory, on the relation of play to ritual, on its philosophical and theological implications, on the psychology of role-playing, and on the philosophy of leisure, I must express extensive obligations to the work of Walter Kaiser, Joseph Pieper, Harvey Cox, Johan Huizinga, Roger Caillois, Jaques Ehrmann, Ernest Kris, Hugo Rahner, William Wimsatt, Herman Hesse, Rudolf Ekstein, Edward Edinger, Conrad Hyers, Ian Donaldson, H.A. Mason, David L. Miller, W. F. Jackson Knight, Sir James G. Frazer, Arnold Stein, Joseph Summers, Mircea Eliade, Thomas Greene, C.R. Deedes, W. H. Matthews, Nathan Scott, and Louis Martz, among others. While many of these authors are specifically cited in text, notes, and bibliography, many are not, and, no doubt, I have overlooked others who have helped to shape my ideas in the ten years I have worked on *Heroic Mockery*.

Seminars at Yale, where farce and epic got a jumbled race, were the proximate cause of this book, which owes much to the acuteness and forebearance of Jim Winn, Naemi

Stilman, Steve Haughney, Melinda Green, Greg Homer, David Bushnell, Deborah Knuth, and David James, among other learned and adventurous young scholars.

Many of my ideas about Minoan myth evolved from discussions in the Aegean and Peloponnesus four years ago with Ferd and Anne La Brunerie, Jamie Oppenheimer, and Susan Peters, who has been a steadfast champion of this book ever since she read an early draft.

In her sophomore year at Yale Nancy Woodington brought extraordinary linguistic and critical talents to bear on the project. When I learned of her facility in German, French, Italian, Dutch, and Latin, I turned her loose on the extensive scholarship about labyrinths and mazes in those languages.

In the decades before and after the turn of the century the labyrinth was subjected to intensive study by continental art historians, archaeologists, anthropologists, and classicists. Thus a learned and highly original study in English, such as W. F. Jackson Knight's *Cumean Gates* or *Vergil's Troy,* while performing an extraordinary task in assimilating many such continental studies, is in a sense but the tip of the iceberg. With Nancy Woodington's help I have sometimes visited its depths, and recollections of works such as G. Q. Giglioli's "L'Oinochoe di Tragliatella," F. Rasch's "De ludo Troiae," Etienne Driston's "La protection magique de Thèbes à l'époque des Ptolémées," Ernst Krause's *Die Trojaburgen Nordeuropas,* F. Muller's "Beteknis van het Labyrinth," and John Layard's "The Labyrinth in the Megalithic Areas of Malekula" perform a mazy dance in my memory.

Penny Marcus, now teaching Italian literature at the University of Texas, lent her wit, critical intelligence, and verve to the evolution of this study in a number of ways, and John Madden found time, despite a double major and other heavy commitments, to help me enormously in transcribing notes I had taped and in tracking down a vast bibliography of studies in epic and mock epic. In the onerous business of securing publishers' permission to quote extensively from works under copyright, Martha Scarf counted many words and wrote many letters without betraying the ennui she must have felt. Perhaps it was a fitting ordeal for a future lawyer.

Among my colleagues at Yale, Mary Reynolds and Mike Seidel have given me invaluable counsel on Joyce, as has David Claus on Homer. Max Byrd has looked over an early draft in the light of his insights into the literature and culture of eighteenth-century England. Maynard Mack has plunged me yet further into a debt that began to accrue nearly forty years ago by scrutinizing an early draft and helping me to bring a curious collocation of ideas into whatever unity and shape it now has. My debt to Robert Fitzgerald is more recent but of the same magnitude. He has read and made invaluable suggestions about three versions of the present study. June Guicharnaud gave the manuscript her expert and sensitive editorial attention. Walter Schindler's judicious reading made me concede, reluctantly, that the final version he read was not the final version. Over the years my friend and colleague, Joel Dorius, has exercised a profound influence on my thinking throughout the book of which he may be unaware, since he has not seen the manuscript.

Sybil Tudor has performed prodigies under pressure in preparing the manuscript for the press.

The officers and editors of Associated University Presses, Inc. and the University of Delaware Press have been the soul of cooperation and diligence. I wish to express my particular thanks to Mr. Ronald B. Roth, who has pursued a complex editorial task with zeal and thoroughness.

To my wife and children, who have suffered with some patience through a number of unsolicited and impromptu lectures on mock heroic, I would like to express my deepest gratitude; more especially to my wife, Ruth, for leading me to the invaluable psychological studies of Rudolf Ekstein, and to my son, George, for preventing me from committing a linguistic howler.

I wish to thank the following publishers for having given me permission to quote from copyrighted material:

Bantam Books, Inc., for permission to quote from THE AENEID OF VIRGIL, translated by Allen Mandelbaum. Translation copyright © 1971 by Allen Mandelbaum. Reprinted by permission of Bantam Books, Inc.

The Bodley Head Ltd., for permission to quote from James Joyce, *Ulysses.*

Chapman & Hall Ltd, for permission to quote from Evelyn Waugh, *Decline and Fall,* 1928.

Faber & Faber, Ltd., for permission to quote from Richard Ellmann, *Ulysses on the Liffey.*

William Heinemann Ltd, for permission to quote from Homer's *Iliad,* translated by Robert Fitzgerald.

International Universities Press, Inc., for permission to quote from Ernst Kris, *Psychoanalytic Explorations in Art.*

Methuen & Co. Ltd, for permission to quote from Alexander Pope, *Poems,* edited by John Butt.

Odyssey Press, Bobbs-Merrill Co., Inc., for permission to quote from *Milton: Complete Poems and Major Prose,* edited by Merritt Y. Hughes.

Oxford University Press, for permission to quote from *The Praise of Folly by Sir Thomas Chaloner,* edited by Clarence H. Miller, The Council of the Early English Text Society, Original Series 257 (1965); and from Richard Ellmann, *Ulysses on the Liffey.*

Random House, Inc., for permission to quote from James Joyce, *Ulysses,* a Modern Library book, Random House, Inc., 1961.

June 1976   G. deF. L.

Introduction

My title, *Heroic Mockery,* is an attempt to avoid the bias inherent in the more familiar term *mock heroic.* Where *mock heroic* usually designates a kind of literature in which the heroic past is used to satirize the contemptible present, this book is principally concerned with literature that criticizes and modifies the heroic tradition or appeals from it to other standards, standards that, while often appearing to be unheroic, attain in the long run a greater validity than those they replace.

English mock heroic appears in its purest form in Dryden's *MacFlecknoe,* where the great tradition of Roman civilization is used to ridicule the achievements of the poet laureate Thomas Shadwell. The glory of Rome and of such successors to its literary traditions as Ben Jonson are seen as beyond reproach, while Shadwell is treated as beneath reproach. The distinctions are absolute and the attack unsparing. In its unqualified reverence for past glories, mock heroic is essentially conservative. Its implicit watchword is, "There were giants in those days," in comparison with which contemporary aspirants to the laurel, oak, or bays are regarded (with the exception of the author and a few friends) as puny wretches.

The characteristic appeal of mock heroic from the dreary present to a glorious past inevitably produced what Louis Bredvold called "the gloom of the Tory satirist."[1] Thus Pope, developing the pattern of *MacFlecknoe* in *The Dunciad,* produced a nightmare vision of contemporary art and letters where not only were words abused, but the Word itself was annihilated. *The Dunciad* marks the ultimate reach of the mock heroic by concluding in self-extinction:

> Lo! thy dread Empire, CHAOS! is restor'd;
> Light dies before thy uncreating word.
> Thy hand, great Anarch! lets the curtain fall;
> And Universal Darkness buries All.

In some respects *The Waste Land* of T.S. Eliot is a prime twentieth-century example of the conservative mock-heroic genre. It mobilizes the glories of classical and biblical myth and legend to expose the spiritual bankruptcy of the modern world. Like *The Dunciad,* it evokes a phantasmagoria of pride, alienation, and triviality in a world so chaotic that coherent utterance is impossible, fragments shored up against the ruins. *The Waste Land,* like *MacFlecknoe* and *The Dunciad,* uses as a central symbol of corruption the polluted Thames and its filthy tributaries, behind which gleams the pristine stream of Spenser's *Prothalamion.* Yet, although *The Waste Land* comes perilously close to the annihilating conclusion of *The Dunciad,* it reserves, at the end of the "Fire Sermon," a glimmer of hope. Unlike *The Dunciad, The Waste Land* ends, not in an apocalyptic catastrophe, but in the possibility of redemption through love, and unlike Pope's protagonist, Eliot's includes himself among the denizens of his nightmare "unreal city." Furthermore, Eliot is not quite so uncritical in his attitude toward the past as Pope: the allusion to Elizabeth and Leicester suggests that even though in Spenser's time the Thames might have been unpolluted, manners were not.

In the "Circe" chapter of Joyce's *Ulysses* the mock-heroic attitude is burlesqued in the character of that renowned *laudator temporis acti,* the Citizen:

> —And our eyes on Europe, says the citizen. We had our trade with Spain and the French and with the Flemings before those mongrels were pupped, Spanish ale in Galway, the wine-bark on the winedark waterway.
> —And will again, says Joe.
> —And with the help of the holy mother of God we will again, says the citizen, clapping his thigh. Our harbors that are empty will be full again, Queenstown, Kinsale, Galway, Blacksod Bay, Ventry in the kingdom of Kerry, Killybegs, the third largest harbour in the wide world with a fleet of masts of the Galway Lynches and the Cavan O'Reillys and the O'Kennedys of Dublin, where the earl of Desmond could make a treaty with the emperor Charles the Fifth himself. And will again, says he, when the first Irish battleship is seen breasting the waves with our own flag to the fore, none of your Henry Tudor's harps, no, the oldest flag afloat, the flag of the province of Desmond and Thomond, three crowns on a blue field, the three sons of Milesius.[2]

Clearly Joyce's mockery implies a more complex and tentative attitude toward tradition versus the contemporary world than the mock heroic usually allows.

Heroic Mockery is chiefly concerned with works of literature that combine Northrop Frye's high-mimetic and low-mimetic modes without finally committing themselves to either one. Unlike *MacFlecknoe* or *The Dunciad,* their thrust is not, finally, satirical, although they inevitably incorporate satire with other modes. Frye sees the history of English literature from the Elizabethan age to the present as a descent from the aristocratic to the bourgeois:

Fictions of romance dominate literature until the cult of the prince and the courtier in the Renaissance brings the high mimetic mode into the foreground. The characteristics of this mode are most clearly seen in the genres of drama, particularly tragedy, and national epic. Then a new kind of middle-class culture introduces the low mimetic which predominates in English literature from Defoe's time to the end of the nineteenth century.[3]

While the transition from high mimetic to low unquestionably defines a major trend in the history of English literature since the Renaissance, my attention will be directed rather to works even more widely separated in time that, in their subtle and often paradoxical amalgamation of high and low, resist Frye's categories. In the earliest and greatest examplars of the high-mimetic mode one finds important elements of low mimetic. The *Odyssey*, while undeniably the archetypal romance, is also—at least in several episodes—the precursor of the bourgeois domestic tale. The extremes of high and low meet and mingle in its versatile hero, the Everyman who assumes the name of Noman, the illustrious warrior-king who, dressed in tatters, is reduced to begging at his own table. Furthermore, in dissolving these conventional antinomies by elevating a shrewd endurance over the aggressiveness and self-assertiveness characteristic of the traditional warrior-hero, Homer anticipates to a certain extent the interdependence of *sublimitas* and *humilitas* at the center of Christian epics like the *Divine Comedy* and *Paradise Lost,* or, to take a quite different kind of development, at the center of Henry Fielding's comic epic in prose.

While the low-mimetic elements in the *Odyssey* are obviously numerous, their presence in the *Iliad* has either been overlooked or misunderstood. The farce of Zeus's seduction by Hera in Book 14, or the indignities suffered by some of the Olympians on the field of battle, or the family squabbles that mar their insouciant symposia, or even the pratfalls suffered by contending heroes in the funeral games in Book 23 have usually been dismissed as tasteless intrusions into the prevailing sublimity and gravity of the poem. Yet when these episodes are seen in the wide context of the *Iliad*'s preoccupation with human mortality, it appears that, far from being trivial or gross, they make an essential contribution to the development of this theme. Thus the *Iliad* incorporates the modes of tragedy, comedy, satire, and farce without being defined or limited by any one of them.

To be more specific, this great example of the high mimetic includes elements of low mimetic that mock its traditional values. An alternation of attitudes toward the heroic code is thus introduced, with the result that the predominant values of the heroic warrior — glorious, egotistical, and tragic — are qualified and, to some extent, superseded by a new kind of heroism — patient, social, and, in a way, fundamentally comic.

In the funeral games for Patroclus, as in the representation on Achilles's shield of the arbitration of a potentially deadly dispute, Homer foreshadows a cultural development whose importance can scarcely be overestimated: the channeling of human aggression into rituals that are not murderous but are compatible with a true civilization. Such a step beyond the rampant individualism of the old warrior-hero is a precondition both to the reestablishment of Odysseus's little kingdom and the founding of imperial Rome.

Crucial to the development from the unrestrained aggressive egotism of the old warrior-hero — of whom the quintessential example is obviously Achilles — to the more amenable, adaptable, and social hero — of whom Odysseus is clearly the archetype — is some manifestation of play. Play avoids the fatal confrontation and provides acceptable alternatives, whether in courts of law, games of chance, or athletic contests. Such playful resolutions of what would otherwise be fatal disputes require each protagonist to accept a substitute gratification for the satisfaction of killing and dishonoring his opponent and appropriating his goods, which, according to contemporary theory, is a type of "zero-sum game," the total gains and losses being calculated to equal zero. (One might question whether such a game doesn't add up to considerably less than zero.) In a play agon, on the other hand, the total gains and losses often amount to considerably more than zero. This is clearly the case in the Homeric games, which confirm the restoration of harmony among the Achaean heroes and their renewed *agapé*.

The transition from the individual pursuit of honor at any cost, as exemplified in Achilles or Hotspur, to the socially controlled pursuit of a less than total victory requires not only a willingness to accept substitutes — the payment of a blood-price instead of the actual blood, the winning of a prize instead of a corpse — but a mutual acceptance by the participants of limits beyond which they agree not to pursue their ambition to win. *Substitution* is related to the "as-if" character of play, while the temporal and spatial limits surrounding it are related to its characteristic lack of consequence (what is sometimes regarded as its unproductive or nonutilitarian quality). In offering to yield his ill-gotten prize to Menelaus, the charioteer Antilochus in *Iliad* 23 realizes that Menelaus's friendship is worth more to him than a prize mare.

Not only does *homo ludens* avoid the deadly consequences of "real" conflicts, but he also attains, if only occasionally and for a moment, a godlike release from mortal care. In the exuberance of their play, Homer's exhausted Achaeans are, for the time being, lifted above the tragedies of everyday life.

If men seek such temporary relief from the consequences of their mortality, those who are forever exempt from them, the Olympians, are continuously in flight from their own inconsequence. Imprisoned by their immortality in an endless round of celestial intrigues, they seek significance through mortal surrogates, thus exemplifying Blake's proverb "Eternity is in love with the productions of Time," since decisive and final action is, ironically enough, the prerogative of mortality. Yet when the Olympians participate either vicariously or directly in battle, consequence eludes them and war becomes just another endless game. Furthermore, without work or death there can be no play, and if leisure, according to the theologian Josef Pieper,[4] is the basis of culture, only mortals can really have it. On the other hand, one might argue that once they have composed their internecine quarrels and reached agreement on important issues like the surrender of Hector's body to Priam or the safe return home of Odysseus, the gods are participating in events of real significance and thereby lending their sanction to crucial cultural developments. It is no accident that before he is willing to surrender Hector's body and accept Priam's ransom, in accordance with the unanimous wish of the gods, Achilles has presided over the games in honor of Patroclus. The principle of *substitution,* which at last permits him to see Hector not only as his enemy but also as his alter ego, and to find in Priam a resemblance to his own aged father, a principle that allows the concessions and compromises essential to society, is embodied in the games — above all, in the chariot race. Substitution helps to circumvent the rigor of the absolute in the heroic code, which demands total victory and total revenge. In agreeing that Achilles should surrender Hector's body and accept the ransom, the Olympians move beyond the daily futility of their existence and acquire dignity and purpose.

"There is no such thing as a feast without gods," according to Josef Pieper.[5] Our literary tradition is nevertheless strewn with ungodly banquets reaching back to those of Thyestes and the impious suitors of Penelope, and extending through the gross collations of Trimalchio, the bottomless consumptions of Gargantua and Falstaff, the Alexandrian revels of Antony and

Cleopatra, to the regimented bad taste of Timon's dinners in Pope's *Epistle to Burlington* or the "pontific luxury" of his gourmandizing priest in the *Dunciad,* or the besotted violence of "the Boller", with which Evelyn Waugh begins *Decline and Fall,* and the memorable extravaganzas on Gatsby's illuminated lawns attended by unheard-of celebrities. As a motif for exposing the corruption of taste and manners, the feast is unexcelled. In its unadulterated form, on the other hand, the feast employs eating, drinking, and festivity to ritualize and consecrate human fellowship and to enhance man's relation to the immortals. Except for the stores he could carry or the game he could kill, the Homeric traveler was absolutely dependent, in a world without inns, on the generosity of strangers. The ambiguity of the Greek *xenos* (guest/friend/stranger) was functional. Until hunger and thirst had been satisfied, the traveler was not asked to identify himself. Thus his only claim to hospitality was that he was a stranger in need of food and drink: this was enough to qualify him as a guest. In the second place, such hospitality was always consecrated with sacrifices to the gods, who were felt to have a particular interest in the protection of strangers. Finally, such feasts, attended by recitals of epic poetry and other kinds of entertainment and by the exchange between host and guest of personal histories, were considered to be the culminating social ritual.

Occasionally the Homeric feast was exuberantly heightened into true revelry. For a time the gravity and sobriety that seem to mark Phaiacian society is laid aside in favor of dances and ball games and other hedonistic contests. At this stage of the feast, the *aoidos* (bard) sets aside his customary repertory of heroic episodes from the war at Troy in favor of the adulterous fabliau involving Ares and Aphrodite and the cuckolded Hephaistos's revenge. Like the sexual comedy of Zeus's beguilement by Hera in *Iliad* 14, this recital has often irritated Homer's critics. Presumably, it was one of the features in

Homer's representation of the gods that excited the disapproval of Plato. Setting aside the moral status of the episode, one can detect in it an element of religious fooling that was to play a major part in the ecclesiastical art and ritual of the High Middle Ages, where customary gravity and discipline were mocked and abrogated in periodic carnivals. In the medieval church these intermittent follies, with their profanities and obscenities, have been defended on the grounds that (1) they are fertility rituals; (2) they serve as a safety valve and, in the long run, contribute to the good order and discipline of the congregation; and (3) the tolerance of such ribaldry in the church calendar testifies to the strength of the orthodox faith. Clearly the boundless *niaiseries* in *Encomium moriae* or *Gargantua and Pantagruel* are no longer regarded by serious readers as reflections on the faith or probity of Erasmus or Rabelais. Why those in Homer should be is an interesting question.

In any case, the blending of folly and festivity has provided some extraordinarily fertile examples of heroic mockery. In many of them the paradoxical relations of high and low mimetic are played with bewildering virtuosity, whether the paradoxes readers are led to are those of Socrates or of St. Paul. Perhaps a major function of the feast of fools is to free the mind from its conventional or habitual attachment to common-sense notions of reality and value, thereby freeing it to respond to the foolishness of God that 1 Corinthians 1:25 tells us is wiser than the wisdom of men.

The festive folly subverts the familiar orders of value in the name of higher orders, such as human brotherhood. The feast of fools tends to emphasize what men share rather than what separates them. From its perspective the number of fools is infinite; the best that anyone can hope for is that he may choose folly of the highest type, such as that which Erasmus's Stultitia treats of in the conclusion of her encomium, the fool in Christ.

While the examples to be considered below, in chapter 3, fall short of the sublime Christian folly of Erasmus, they exemplify various secular versions of the theme and attain a profound and scintillatingly complex intermingling of high and low mimetic. Where the dialectic of games concludes by establishing new standards, the paradoxes in the feast of fools may be left in an uneasy and irresolute balance, as in the case of *Antony and Cleopatra,* where at most one can only conclude that in some way the self-destructive folly of the lovers is preferable to the calculating efficiency of Fortune's Fool, Octavius. Even to do this is to make a personal choice and to ignore the social and political points of view that continually qualify the personal or romantic perspective. If one tries to maintain that the Alexandrian festivities are nourishing and life-enhancing rituals, one must also concede that they are wasteful orgies. Thus Egyptian Epicureanism mocks Roman Stoicism, but it is mocked by it in turn. Perhaps in combining the best of both virtues in their deaths, the lovers succeed in shackling accident and bolting up change, thereby ending the hateful siege of contraries, but even here the reader has to take Cleopatra's word for it.

If the secular feast of fools leads to a dilemma of fascinating imaginative power, as Shakespearean criticism testifies, it leaves us in the midst of a maze of paradoxes and contradictions. The alternatives of public and personal satisfactions and responsibilities are so nicely balanced for Antony that no right course of action is available to him. This plight is quite unlike the plight of Aeneas in Book 4. Aeneas's destiny leaves no doubt as to where his duty lies, but Antony is not directed by Heaven to perform a heroic imperial task. In contrast to the degeneracy of politics, the love of Cleopatra seems worthy of a hero, but then, of course, she betrays him (after his political marriage) — or does she? The bases by which duty is determined in *Antony and Cleopatra* are not clear and firm, as in the

Aeneid, but shifting and hypothetical. At the climax Cleopatra projects onto the maze of motives and values the myth by which she dies, but even this may be a delusion.

In the next chapter I shall attempt to show how an ancient myth is employed by Joyce to escape from the dilemma created by such conflicts of subjective values and myths. In Joyce's use of the myth of the Minoan labyrinth, paradox reconciles contraries instead of leaving them in irreconcilable contradictions or irresolution. In doing so, Joyce returns to the fundamentals of the ancient myth. The essential meanings he finds in the Daedalian labyrinth are explicitly and implicitly present in the versions of Homer, Virgil, and Ovid. In its completed form the myth of Daedalus brings together the experiences of falling into sin, of descent into a place of darkness and punishment, of a mystical encounter, and, finally, of deliverance. The labyrinthine movement. downward and upward through twin gyres is the only pattern that can interrelate the apparently conflicting movments upward and downward and away from and toward the center. Furthermore, the labyrinth, like the Möbius strip, provides a continuous and uninterrupted movement from one face to its opposite. The outside becomes the inside as one moves, and vice versa. The rigid oppositions characteristic of ordinary experience are thereby dissolved or reconciled. In Minoan architecture and the consecrating rituals that lay behind it, the labyrinth and the related spiral exemplified a controlled apotropaic function. The labyrinth could thus exclude strangers while permitting the initiates to enter.

As Joyce employs the labyrinth, it provides a continuum from low to high and from high to low. Joyce regards error (a key word in Virgil's labyrinth) as a precondition to freedom, thus overriding the conventional discontinuities and oppositions between up and down, vice and virtue, noble and ignoble, and so forth. The labyrinth continuum obviously has its counterpart in Joyce's style, especially in *Ulysses*, where the dissolution of the normal categories of high and low mimetic is reflected in an idiom and rhetoric that can, at times, produce mock-heroic incongruities, but that ultimately see high and low as inseparably related to each other in man's fate. The Minoan labyrinth that Joyce adapted so sensitively from the great writers of antiquity provides a new kind of comic epic in which the central myths of the *Odyssey* and the *Metamorphoses* are brought into a brilliant and fertile conjunction.

HEROIC MOCKERY

I

Heroic Games

> There was no "One, two, three, and away!", but
> they began running when they liked, and left off
> when they liked, so that it was not easy to know
> when the race was over. However, when they had
> been running half an hour or so, and were quite dry
> again, the Dodo suddenly called out "The race is
> over!" and they all crowded round it, panting, and
> asking "But who has won?"
> — Lewis Carroll, *Alice's Adventures in Wonderland*

The high point of Evelyn Waugh's brilliant satirical novel
Decline and Fall (New York: Dell, 1959) is without doubt the
games held at Llanabba School, a worm-eaten, pseudo-Gothic
establishment in Wales that seems to be dedicated to ignorance,
mendacity, and pretentiousness. The games, or sports, as
Waugh calls them, display all the essential features of an athletic tradition reaching back through the first Olympiad to the
prime model, the games that Achilles ordains to memorialize

Patroclus in Book 23 of the *Iliad,* but in every detail the ideals
that lie behind heroic games are corrupted, thwarted, or
mocked.

Augustus Fagan, D.D., Llanabba's headmaster, proclaims
the sports on the eve of a visit from wealthy and prestigious
parents, such as the Countess of Circumference and Lady
Margot Beste-Chetwynde. While he declares them to be an
annual event, it appears that they occur only on such occasions.
The preparations are so hasty that the preliminary heats are as
yet incomplete when they are reported in the local paper. The
referee for the relay races is an incompetent master named
Prendergast. In the preliminary heats he sends wave after wave
of racers off into the cold rain of a dark Welsh afternoon,
but none ever returns:

> "Well," asked Paul, "how are the sports going?"
> "Not very well," said Mr. Prendergast; "in fact, they've
> gone."
> "All over?"
> "Yes. You see, none of the boys came back from the first
> race. They just disappeared behind the trees at the top of
> the drive. I expect they've gone to change. I don't blame
> them, I'm sure. It's terribly cold. Still it was discouraging
> launching heat after heat and none coming back. Like send-
> ing troops into battle." (P. 273).

The Llanabba games are, in fact, antigames. Perhaps
"un-games" is a better word. Everywhere they tacitly invoke
the traditional standards of heroic games, of fair play, of the
joy of effort, of endurance, of team spirit, of honor, only to
flout them. Beyond these corruptions and violations lies something even more inimical to the essence of games. As Johan
Huizinga says, the real enemy of games is not the cheat but the
spoilsport, for the cheat usually attempts to appear to observe
the rules, while the spoilsport can destroy the game by simply

refusing to play.[1] This trenchant observation leads one close to
the center of Waugh's satirically conceived contests. They are
"un-games," games that have been exhausted of meaning
because the circumstances without which there can be no
games are clearly lacking. A fundamental requisite for any
athletic contrast is that it be subject to spatial and temporal
limits. Since a race with a starting point but no finish line is
clearly not a race, Prendergast's deserters are as absurd as the
students who compete for Pennyfeather's prize for "the longest
essay, irrespective of any possible merit," to be written on the
theme of "self-indulgence" (p. 254). Yet the deserters are not,
finally, absurd, because they seem to intuit that whatever they
do, there will be no true games. And they are right, since the
distribution of prizes has been determined beforehand, "irrespective of any possible merit," by the headmaster's instruc-
tions: "And, Pennyfeather, I hope you will see that they are
distributed fairly evenly about the school. It doesn't do to let
any boy win more than two events; I leave you to arrange that.
I think it would be only right if little Lord Tangent won something, and Beste-Chetwynde—yes, his mother is coming down,
too" (p. 265). "Fairly" and "evenly" here take on unaccustom-
ed meanings in the tradition of gamesmanship. Dr. Fagan is
staging a spectacle that will leave with the uninitiated or naive
participant or spectator the illusion that he is competing in or
watching real games, while the reader is privy to the hilariously
sordid manipulations behind the scenes, as in the following
episode:

Grimes was in the Common Room.
"Just back from the gay metropolis of Llandudno," he
said. "Shopping with Dingy is not a seemly occupation for a
public-school man. How did the heats go?"
"There weren't any," said Paul.
"Quite right," said Grimes; "you leave this to me. I've

been in the trade some time. These things are best done over the fire. We can make out the results in peace. We'd better hurry. The old boy wants them sent to be printed this evening."

And taking a sheet of paper and a small stub of pencil, Grimes made out the programme.

"How about that?" he said.

"Clutterbuck seems to have done pretty well," said Paul.

"Yes, he's a splendid little athlete," said Grimes. (P. 273)

The corrupted games take place within a circle of more extensive rivalries, as the unspeakable Grimes's allusion to what is or is not suitable for a public-school man suggests. The occasion for the games is really to flatter Margot Beste-Chetwynde and Lady Circumference, whose goodwill can lend Llanabba badly needed *ton*. Social emulation in *Decline and Fall* is even more spurious than the athletic rivalries of the schoolboys. "Without the gods there are no feasts," and, accordingly, the patron deity of the Llanabba sports, Margot, the Venus of a chapter entitled *Pervigilium Veneris,* appears to have poisoned her husband and is later revealed to be the operator of a vast international chain of bordellos.

If the games are implicitly dedicated to Margot in somewhat the way that the Homeric and Virgilian contests are dedicated to various Olympians, they are presided over by a hero of the counterculture whose manners and values correspond in a skewed way to those of Achilles in *Iliad* 23 or Aeneas in *Aeneid* 5. The relationship is usually an inversion of heroic values, a moral bankruptcy that intermittently masks itself to the audience and lifts the mask to the initiated reader. At times Dr. Fagan is carried away by the exuberance of his own verbosity. The thought of flowers for Lady Circumference sets off a whole train of festive associations: " 'You are to procure the most expensive bouquet that Wales can offer; do you understand? Flowers, youth, wisdom, the glitter of jewels,

music. . .*And fireworks*,' said the Doctor" (p. 264). In more
sober and revealing moments, however, the learned Doctor
shows himself to be the inveterate foe of games, sports, or any
other manifestations of culture: "I can think of no entertainment that fills me with greater detestation than a display of
competitive athletics, none—except possibly folk-dancing" (p.
275). Yet just as the attitude of Achilles or Aeneas toward the
games they conduct tells a great deal about their attitude
toward life in general, so that the games become reflectors of
more extended realities, Fagan's hatred of the School's sports is
a perfect image of his aversion to the School itself and life in
general. When, in interviewing Paul Pennyfeather for a posi-
tion as master at Llanabba, he learns that the candidate has
been sent down from Oxford for moral turpitude, his compo-
sure is unshaken. He simply uses the information as grounds
for reducing Pennyfeather's future salary, while observing:

> "I have been in the scholastic profession long enough to
> know that nobody enters it unless he has some very good
> reason which he is anxious to conceal. But, again to be prac-
> tical, Mr. Pennyfeather, I can hardly pay one hundred and
> twenty pounds to anyone who has been sent down for inde-
> cent behavior. Suppose we fix your salary at ninety pounds
> a year to begin with?" (P. 236)

Much recent writing on the theory and sociology of play
has stressed the importance of freedom in authentic games.
The participants must be volunteers and they must be amateurs,
according to some purists. Among virtually all writers there is
agreement that the world of games is set apart from the workaday world. A fête like that at Llanabba occurs in a special
time, set apart from customary quotidian occupations. Often
the distinction is made between games and "real life" or
"work." For the most part, theoretical approaches discover in
games a ritual function that brings them at times close to the

sacred. The court or field in which they take place and the rules that govern them are seen as having some of the hallowed quality of temples or courts of law. This set-apart character is a feature stressed in most theoretical discussions of games, whether philosophical, historical, psychological, anthropological, or theological. In this respect, and in the wider context of theories of play in general, games can provide mortals, within strictly observed spatial and temporal limits, with a momentary holiday from the iron necessities of daily life. For a while the rapt player is exempt from the pressures of time and enjoys in his brief holiday a kind of immortal status. Some kinds of play elevate the human to the divine.

A surprisingly large number of these assumptions is implicit in Waugh's *Decline and Fall,* though slanted for satirical purposes. The generosity that characterizes Achilles, Aeneas, and other heroic regisseurs is spoiled by a cheese-paring calculus that allows refreshments only to influential guests. The theatrical element in Dr. Fagan's games is reflected in his concern for effects and his utter disregard for values. He is a cinema director, instructing his prop-man: "and, Pennyfeather, if you would with tact direct the photographer so that more prominence was given to Mrs. Beste-Chetwynde's Hispano-Suiza than to Lady Circumference's little motor car, I think it would all be to the good. All these things count, you know" (p. 277). Such effects "count" with the doctor, but he is quite indifferent to the fact that the "ground" has not been marked and that the hurdles are spiked iron railings, oversights that he dismisses imperturbably with the announcement that "the prizes had been previously competed for" (p. 277).

Even more central to the nature of Waugh's "un-game" is the drastic confusion in which "play" is confounded by "reality." In the interests of "style," one of his favorite concerns, Dr. Fagan requires that the races begin with a starting pistol, duly produced by the villainous butler, Philbrick, who warns him that it is loaded. Prendergast, the starter, who has somehow managed to get excessively drunk, accidentally shoots little Lord Tangent in the foot, a wound of which he later dies. It would be hard to conceive of a more striking image for the encroachment of the "real" world on the "play" world. It has some of the force of the familiar line, "And wretches hang that jurymen may dine," without any of the explicit moral concern. " 'Am I going to die?' said Tangent, his mouth full of cake. . . 'First blood to me!' said Mr. Prendergast gleefully" (p. 285). In a curious turnabout, the play world of *Decline and Fall* is sometimes fraught with fatal consequences that are normally limited to the "real world," while the "real world" of the book has some of the godlike inconsequentiality that we usually find in the "play" world. For example, all the characters of any importance, however irresponsible or wicked, are virtually untouched by experience. Hence the book is constructed as a series of cartoons. Its episodic structure is virtually dictated by Waugh's conception of his characters — or Olympians — moving from episode to episode without suffering any change or undergoing any development. For the character development in ordinary fiction Waugh substitutes metamorphosis of roles. Philbrick has a repertory of semifictional autobiographies that could outdo in variety and scope that master of the heroic lie, Odysseus. And Pennyfeather, perhaps the most passive central intelligence that ever graced a novel, finds himself, after an incredible series of misadventures, back in the comfortable world of Scone College, from which he had been catapulted at the beginning of the book. The only difference is the name of the friend with whom he discusses a paper read in the League of Nations Union: Potts has become Stubbs.

The archetypal games of *Iliad* 23 and their numerous imitations in the epic tradition serve to modulate the ambition and egotism of the competing heroes and reintegrate them into a more harmonious relationship with each other. Homer arranges things so that nobody's status is damaged by the preeminence of a winner. Achilles' even-handed judgement, while recognizing the heroic worth of winners, also celebrates the virtues of runners-up and (in a celebrated case, that of Nestor) even of those who are no longer young enough to compete. The recognition of merit is thus tempered by affectionate regard for the individual. In the *Iliad* this results in a great increase of mutual respect and goodwill among the Achaeans. The values of intense competition are tempered by knowledge that the worth of an individual may be expressed in many different ways, some of them incapable of demonstration or proof on the playing field. Judgment, based on the objective test, is tempered by a merciful regard for the unique virtues of the individual.

In contrast, the games at Llanabba conclude on a note of mutual rancor. The festival functions as a disintegrating anti-ritual from which no one emerges with any *areté* (heroic excellence). In the final race young Clutterbuck (who has already been assigned three prizes in previous pseudoevents) contrives to come in at the head of the pack by lurking out of sight before the last lap:

> Round and round the muddy track trotted the athletes while the silver band played sacred music unceasingly.
> "Last lap!" announced Paul.
> The school and the visitors crowded about the tape to cheer the winner. Amid loud applause Clutterbuck breasted the tape well ahead of the others.
> "Well run! Oh, good, jolly good, sir!" cried Colonel Sidebotham.
> "Well run, Percy!" chorused the two little Clutterbucks, prompted by their governess.
> "That boy cheated," said Lady Circumference. "He only went round five times. I counted."
> "I think unpleasantness so mars the afternoon," said the Vicar.

"How dare you suggest such a thing?" asked Mrs. Clutter-buck. "I appeal to the referee. Percy ran the full course, didn't he?"

"Clutterbuck wins," said Captain Grimes.

"Fiddlesticks!" said Lady Circumference. "He deliberately lagged behind and joined the others as they went behind the benches. The little toad!"

"Really, Greta," said Lord Circumference, "I think we ought to abide by the referee's decision."

"Well, they can't expect me to give away the prizes, then. Nothing would induce me to give that boy a prize."

"Do you understand, madam, that you are bringing a serious accusation against my son's honour?"

"Serious accusation fiddlesticks! What he wants is a jolly good hidin'." (P. 287)

Dr. Fagan's intervention in the dispute at this point is a masquerade of justice:

At this stage of the discussion the Doctor left Mrs. Hope-Browne's side, where he had been remarking upon her son's progress in geometry, and joined the group round the winning post.

"If there is a disputed decision," he said genially, "they shall race again."

"Percy has won already," said Mr. Clutterbuck. "He has been adjudged the winner."

"Splendid! splendid! A promising little athlete. I congratulate you, Clutterbuck."

"But he only ran five laps," said Lady Circumference.

"Then clearly he has won the five furlong race, a very exacting length."

"But the other boys," said Lady Circumference, almost beside herself with rage, "have run six lengths."

"Then they," said the Doctor imperturbably, "are first, second, third, and fourth, respectively in the Three Miles. Clearly there has been some confusion. Diana, I think we might now serve tea." (P. 288)

Blandly indifferent to time, distance, and number, as well as the contestants' merit (or lack of it), the headmaster confounds reason and perpetrates the ultimate violation of the game.

Whether or not Evelyn Waugh intended the Llanabba School Games as a parody of the games in the *Iliad*, the mock-heroic episode in *Decline and Fall* and the heroic games in the *Iliad* are mutually illuminating, even in the smallest details. Of the eight events in Homer the chariot race, by far the richest and most significant, shares in various ways all the features of Waugh's race. A truce has been declared, so that customary hostilities between Achaeans and Trojans are suspended. The games are prefaced by a feast. Achilles, who proclaims the games and judges the contests, provides the prizes in profusion. He sets the goal and marks out the course. The contestants volunteer for the event (instead of being conscripted, as Waugh's little athletes are). Antilochus, like Clutterbuck, is guilty of cheating, or, at least, of unsportsmanlike sharp practice. There is a furious dispute, but rather than ignore the issues, Achilles helps to resolve it. The event ends with rancor dissipated and mutual respect and affection enhanced.

Stimulated by the advice of his old father, Nestor, Antilochus cuts out Menelaus at the turning point of the race. In this game of "chicken," Menelaus's nerve fails him, and he reins in his horses to avoid a collision, so that Antilochus reaches the finish line ahead of him, first place having been won without challenge by Diomedes. The dispute begins with Achilles' suggestion that the second prize go to Eumelos, who was forced to drop out of the race because his chariot broke down. Achilles, who "takes pity" on Eumelos as he leads his horses and broken chariot across the finish line, declares (from *The Iliad: Homer*, trans. Robert Fitzgerald [Garden City, N.Y.: Anchor Press/Doubleday, 1974]):

The best man is the last to bring his team in.
Come, we'll award him second prize, in fairness.
Let Diomedes have the first.

(23.536-38)

All the Achaeans approve the decision except Antilochus, who objects:

O Akhilleus,
if you go through with this thing you've announced,
I'll be furious! You mean to take my prize,
considering that his chariot and team
were hurt, and he, too, the brave fellow. Well
he should have prayed the immortals! If he had,
he would have finished far from last. Granted
that you are sorry for him, fond of him,
there's gold aplenty in your hut, and bronze,
and you have cattle, serving maids, and horses.
Take some later; give him a greater prize;
or take them here and now. You'll have the Akhaians'
praise for it.

(23.543-52)

Even more indignant and intransigent than Lady Circumference, he concludes with a deadly threat, *"I will not yield the mare./ And any man who cares to fight for her/can try me, hand to hand"* (23.553-54).

Achilles, "enjoying Antilokhos, as he liked the man," now proposes another consolation prize for Eumelos and is on the point of awarding the mare to Antilochus, when "Menelaos /faced them all, still sore at heart, his anger/grimly set against Antilokhos. A herald/handed him a staff and called for silence" (23.566-69). The detail of the scepter, which entitles the speaker to be heard, underlines the seriousness of Menelaus's appeal to justice and fair play. He accuses Antilochus of fouling him and offers him a chance to exonerate himself under oath. Thus the dispute, instead of being left beclouded

by rancor or aggravated by angry claims, is put to the
judgment of the Argive counsellors:

> Antilokhos, come here, sir, as good discipline
> requires; stand there before your team and car.
> Pick up the slim whip that you used in driving;
> touch your horses; by the god of earthquake
> swear you did not mean to foul my car.

(23.581-85)

In a remarkable comic peripeteia, Antilochus judges his
own behavior with "You know a young man may go out of
bounds" and acknowledges his "judgment" as "slight" (23.589-
590):

> Be patient, then. The mare I won I'll give you,
> and any other and greater thing of mine
> you might request I'd wish to give at once,
> rather than fall in your esteem, my lord,
> for all my days, and live as an offender
> before the unseen powers.

(23.590-94)

The dispute is now transformed into a contest of mutual
regard. Antilochus leads the mare up and gives her to Menelaus.
But Menelaus's anger is softened "as growing grain is, when
ears shine with dew/and the fields ripple" (23.598-99). The
simile, occurring in an episode otherwise nearly devoid of
them, marks a truly striking shift in the attitudes of the two
men. Justice, mutual respect, and affection nourish and foster
the relations among men. The bitter wrangle over the mare
now turns into a delightful Alphonse-Gaston competition in
generosity, as Menelaus, while noting that she is properly
his, bestows her on Antilochus and accepts the prize for third
place. His concluding words are worth close attention:

                              Now,
Antilokhos, I am coming round to you,
after my anger. You were never thoughtless
before this. Youth prevailed over your good sense.
The next time, have a care not to pull tricks
on higher officers. Truly no other
Akhaian could so quickly win me over,
but you've fought hard, and toiled long years,
as your father and brave brother have, for me.
I shall comply with what you asked at first
and give the mare to you, though she is mine,
so these men too may know
my temper is not cruel and overbearing.

                                        (23.601-11)

In depth of insight and strength and delicacy of feeling the exchange between these two heroes is infinitely richer than the famous and much-discussed speeches between Glaucus and Sarpedon in *Iliad* 12. Menelaus's concluding speech, more than any other passage in the *Iliad*, establishes precisely and clearly the fundamentals of a proper relationship between heroes, allies, and men of goodwill. Without in any way overlooking Antilochus's breach of fair play, he pardons it partly on the grounds of the offender's youth, but principally — and touchingly — on the grounds of the sacrifices that Antilochus and his family have made on Menelaus's behalf, a generous recognition that Agamemnon is too obtuse to make.

In the dispute and reconciliation between these two heroes the desire to win is tempered by a recognition on both sides that winning is not everything. A primitive principle that underlies the conventional heroic code is the kudos of being number one, even if that entails disgrace or humiliation for one's rival. This drive for preeminence, which Shakespeare was to explore so brilliantly in the character of Hotspur in 1 *Henry IV*, clearly derives from a conception of honor in

battle won at the expense of the loser. As the dying Hotspur
says to the prince, "I better brook the loss of brittle life/Than
those proud titles thou hast won of me."[2] Behind that
rivalry, as behind heroic emulation in the *Iliad*, there seems to
lie the notion that there is a fixed amount of honor to be had,
which is to be got only at the expense of somebody else.
In contemporary theory, as seen earlier, this is called a zero-
sum game. When it is translated into the terms of the battlefield, it might be regarded as a game adding up to considerably
less than zero, since the acquisition of honor by one hero
usually entails not only the loss of honor by the loser, but the
loss of life as well. By way of a drastic modification of the
economics of the agon, Homer establishes a new kind of game
in which the honor of both participants, of winner and loser
alike, is enhanced. In fact, one cannot tell who wins or who
loses. And actually, everyone wins, not only in the chariot
race but in the other events as well, since there are prizes
for all the contestants and even for some noncontestants. Thus
Achilles, with an extra prize on his hands, awards it to the
aged Nestor and is rewarded in turn by a moving, if prolix,
speech of appreciation. After recollecting his youthful achievements at the funeral games for Amaryngkeus, Nestor concludes:

> That was the man I was. Now let the young
> take part in these exertions: I must yield
> to slow old age, though in my time I shone
> among heroic men.
>   Well, carry on
> the funeral of your friend with competitions.
> This I take kindly, and my heart is cheered
> that you remember me as well disposed,
> remembering, too, the honor that is due me
> among Akhaians. May the gods
> in fitting ways reward you for it all.

(23.643-50)

Two points should be made here. The first is that Nestor wishes happiness to an Achilles who knows that his death is imminent; hence the situation is full of unwitting tragic irony. Secondly, the situation is at the same time full of unwitting comic irony. It was Nestor, after all, whose suggestions about strategy induced his son to foul Menelaus, so that the fault ultimately was not due to youthful indiscretion, as Menelaus supposed and as Antilochus admitted, but to the machinations of this ancient repository of wisdom! What could have been merely a somewhat sentimental expression of *agapé*, as in the episode of Nisus and Euryalus in Virgil's games, is here toughened by the irony with which it is alloyed. In the race of life Achilles knows that this senescent hero will survive him, but he has now reached a kind of illumination toward his own doom, "a lightning before death," as Romeo calls it in *Romeo and Juliet* (5.3.90). Without further words, "when he had listened to all the praise spoken," Achilles returns to his seat and proceeds with the next event.

The Homeric games are suffused with intimations of mortality, above all in the case of Achilles. Not only are they in honor of a dead friend who embodied almost everything Achilles cared about, but Achilles is fully aware that his killing of his friend's killer, Hector, has brought his own death closer. The honor he has achieved is inseparable from his doom, and the option that was once his of a long, happy life, but without honor, is no longer open to him. The games he conducts with such skill, fairness, and affection ritualize his profound reappraisal of the heroic code of glory. Where once he wished, like Hotspur, to wear "without corrival all the dignities" of honor, he now presides over a distribution of honor; he has discovered a new economics of honor. For the old economics of scarcity he has substituted an economics of abundance whose primary law is that, in the good heroic society, no individual need be ruined by another's success.

Earlier, he had expressed a more primitive view of honor to Patroclus:

> Ah, Father Zeus, Athena, and Apollo!
> If not one Trojan of them all
> should get away from death, and not one Argive
> save ourselves were spared, we two alone
> could pull down Troy's old coronet of towers!

(16.97-100)

The rules of the game and the way in which Achilles administers them are ultimately a response to the pressure of mortality in the *Iliad*. The spatial and temporal limits characteristic of all true games not only provide a respite from the daily burdens of existence, manifested in the *Iliad* by the mounting toll of casualties, but serve as well to minimize the accidental inequalities of life. Where brute strength alone can win a battle, which is true for an Ajax or a Teucer, a greater variety of skills and virtues comes into play in the games. Thus when Odysseus's "craft" offsets Ajax's superior muscle and they wrestle to a draw (23.700-737), Achilles declares that they both have won. On the other hand, despite the function of games in equalizing opportunities for the contestants, accidents that might prove fatal in battle sometimes occur. Allowance is made for chance (*tuché*) and fortune, sometimes in the guise of a favoring deity. Eumelos's mishap in the chariot race Antilochus has attributed to his failure to "pray the immortals," and Athene is said to help Odysseus in the footrace. Yet, as E. R. Dodds demonstrated some time ago,[3] a divine intervention on behalf of mortals in Homer usually coincides with an act of will by the individual who is helped. In the footrace the other Ajax, the foul-mouthed and disputatious son of Oïleus, loses through the gross mischance of slipping on the dung of a sacrificial bull. Spitting the dung from his mouth, Ajax attributes his defeat by Odysseus to the goddess " always beside him, like a coddling mother.'/At this the crowd laughed at him, full of glee" (23.782-84). And while behind this mischance there are traces of poetic justice, one can also see it as a comic version of what are often fatal mischances in real life. The incident in a comic way reveals the intrusion of down-to-earth reality into the sequestered world of play, much as does the grimmer farce of Lord Tangent's being shot in the foot. Indeed the threatening encroachment of reality upon the play world seems to be a feature of heroic and mock-heroic festivities.

While the games provide a holiday from real life, they also provide a great deal more. Granted that within their limits they give participants and onlookers alike a brief respite from the pressures of mortality, that they ritualize the "unsaying" of Achilles' anger and help to restore harmony to the Achaeans, their greatest significance is in recapitulating the tragic quarrel with which the *Iliad* begins. I have dwelt on the chariot race in Book 23 at length because I am convinced that it is a comic reworking of the quarrel. The trouble all started in a dispute between Achilles and Agamemmon over prizes. Because Agamemnon insisted on keeping the daughter of Chryses, the priest of Apollo, Apollo sent a plague upon the Achaeans. A council called by Achilles urges Agamemnon to return the girl, which he reluctantly agrees to do with the proviso that he will take in compensation Briseis, the prize of Achilles. Although Agamemnon has insisted that he loves Chryseis, Chryses' daughter, it is clear that not love but some kind of *amour-propre* is at issue, as his angry speech to Achilles indicates:

> What do you really ask? That you may keep
> your own winnings, I am to give up mine
> and sit here wanting her? Oh, no:
> the army will award a prize to me

and make sure that it measures up, or if
they do not, I will take a girl myself,
your own, or Aias', or Odysseus' prize!
Take her, yes, to keep. The man I visit
may choke with rage; well, let him.

(1.133-39)

These extraordinarily offensive remarks lead Achilles to remind
Agamemnon that he and his allies had suffered no injury
from the Trojans when they joined the expedition to Troy.

No, no, we joined for you, you insolent boor,
to please you, fighting for your brother's sake
and yours, to get revenge upon the Trojans.
You overlook this, dogface, or don't care,
and now in the end you threaten to take my girl,
a prize I sweated for, and soldiers gave me!

(1.157-62)

The prize is important to Achilles but not nearly so important
as Agamemnon's obtuse incapacity to recognize and appreciate
the sacrifices of his allies, who have no personal stake in the
quarrel. Agamemnon's grasping insecurity and monumental
coarseness of sensibility, coupled with dreadfully bad judgment,
make him a worthy predecessor to a long line of high-ranking
military boobs, culminating in Herman Wouk's Captain Queeg
and Joseph Heller's Colonel Korn, Colonel Cathcart, and General
Dreedle. This situation is inverted in Menelaus's honorable
and generous speech to Antilochus in Book 23. As in that
quarrel, where Antilochus utters a threat to kill anyone who
tries to take his prize, Achilles is now on the verge of drawing
his sword and killing the chief, but Athene restrains him,
suggesting that he can punish him more effectively by with-
drawing from the fight. Seizing the scepter to solemnize his
words, as Menelaus does in the other episode, Achilles now
swears an irrevocable oath not to come to Agamemnon's aid

when the Achaians "perish before/the killer, Hektor" (1.242-
43). Further to confirm his irreversible decision, Achilles
compares it to

> this great staff: look: leaf or shoot
> it cannot sprout again, once lopped away
> from the log it left behind in the timbered hills;
> it cannot flower, peeled of bark and leaves;
> instead, Akhaian officers in council
> take it in hand by turns, when they observe
> by the will of Zeus due order in debate.
>
> (1.234-44)

Thus the central image of the fatal schism between Achilles
and Agamemnon is the irremediable death of what was once
"a great rooted blossomer." The corresponding image at the
center of the encounter between Menelaus and Antilochus is,
as shown above, ripening grain. And, of course, it is this
scepter that Menelaus holds when he asks Antilochus to swear
that he has not cheated in the chariot race. There, as well
as here, it is a symbol of the justice (*themis*) of Zeus. In
dashing it to the ground at the end of his furious oath,
Achilles seems to be gesturing against the injustice of Agamemnon. Indeed, as one learns in Book 2, it is Agamemnon's
scepter, and it has a tragic history, having been made by
Hephaistos for Zeus, who gave it to Hermes. From Hermes it
descended through the nightmare of Argive history, through
Pelops, Atreus, and Thyestes, to Agamemnon. Its provenience
recapitulates generations of bloody feuds and gross injustices,
culminating in Agamemnon's brute act of theft and leading
ultimately to a "stiff, dishonored shroud" in Argos. The scepter,
then, is at once a symbol of the justice of Zeus and a symbol
of the violations of which each successive chief of the Pelopidae
and Atreidae has been guilty. While Agamemnon is clearly
guilty of abusing the *themis* for which it stands, his brother,

in Book 23, employs it properly to enforce a just resolution of the quarrel. In a larger context Achilles' dashing of the scepter to the ground manifests his bitter awareness that under this king there are no rules. Since his honor has been ruthlessly violated, the war to recover the honor of the Atreidae is an absurdity. He has no choice but to withdraw.

The absurdity of the situation deepens when it becomes clear that the sole justification for the Achaian attack against Troy is to punish the rape of Helen and to get her back. If the chief champion of the crusaders ravishes his officer's woman, what does that do to the whole Greek cause? Paris, at least, was swayed by passion, but Agamemnon is easily consoled for the loss of Chryseis, whose name, triply rhyming with that of her substitute, Briseis, implies that the girls are for him, at least, as indistinguishable as Sansloy and Sansfoy or the two beauties in Spenser's fountain.

Furthermore, this comic irony — comic only in the immediate context — is overshadowed by a much more complex tragic irony. Agamemnon has unwittingly woven for himself the net that will symbolize his doom in Aeschylus's tragedy. But far more ominous is the doom that Achilles has unintentionally prepared for himself by seeking revenge through Achaian losses. Those, he knows, will enhance his importance. What he does not know is that they will culminate in the death of the one person whose companionship makes the bitterness of his life endurable. Thus Agamemnon, acting on a false economics of honor, precipitates a catastrophic process by which no one can win. The process moves remorselessly from death to death, until, under the terrible pressure of his comrades' losses, Achilles reluctantly agrees to let Patroclus enter the battle in his armor. When he slays Sarpedon, the ineluctable trap is set. In revenge for *his* friend, Hector slays Patroclus. In revenge for *his*, Achilles slays Hector, who is wearing the old Achillean armor stripped from Patroclus, a detail that nicely symbolizes the suicidal nature of Achilles' act, the necessary prelude to his own death. Nothing could express more succinctly or vividly the self-destructive potential of the quest for honor in the heroic game of war.

To return once more to the games in *Iliad* 23, it should be emphasized that the quarrel between Antilochus and Menelaus, who are surrogates for Agamemnon and Achilles in Book 1, reflects the tragic dispute of Book 1, but the tragedy is averted by way of a fair and honorable adjudication of the issue and, more particularly, by the willingness of both principals to honor justice, which means observing the "rules of the game." Agamemnon's proud intransigence expressed in his emphatic refusal to return Chryseis (1.29), echoed in Antilochus's refusal to give up his prize, *"I will not yield the mare"* (23.553), is the first step in a series of fatally irreversible speeches and actions. While it is true that, like Antilochus, he yields on this point, his insistence on taking Achilles' prize is catastrophic. What Antilochus introduces into the *Iliad* is a willingness to abandon intransigent defiance under the sanctions of justice, while realizing that in yielding he can gain far more than he could by defiance. In the game world such blessed peripeties can flourish.

Finally, it is not too much to claim that in their fullest implications the funeral games for Patroclus mark a vital step forward in the rise of civilization. The heroic code, with its feudlike dialectic of revenge and its narrow conception of honor, cannot be a firm foundation for society. Even if the ideal of *timé* (honor) is scrupulously observed, it is a fundamentally divisive and egotistical ideal. Nor is the avenging of wrongs *vi et armis* a deterrent to repeated acts of outrage on either side. Like the fatal chain that links Achilles' doom to Hector's, Hector's to Patroclus's, and Patroclus's to Sarpedon's, the rape of Helen leads to the sacking of Troy and the desecration of the citadel of Pallas Athene, which leads in turn to the death of Ajax, son of Oïleus, and the ten years' harrassment of Odysseus. In the meantime Agamemnon's sacrifice of Iphigenia at Aulis (unmentioned in Homer) may to some extent provide a motive for his murder by Clytemnestra. Thus the bloody chain of "necessity" adds link to link until it is broken, at least for a while, by Aeneas's victory over Turnus and the establish- ment of the *Pax Romana*. The games in *Iliad* 23 intimate an entirely different basis for a peaceful society from that imposed by the military force of Rome. Homeric society, far less complex than that which Virgil knew, could nevertheless occasionally express the rudiments of a social ideal in some respects light-years ahead of Virgil's, one founded on justice, mutual respect, and, most importantly, a willingness to submit disputes to arbitration.

Achilles' shield represents, among other pairs of contrasting vignettes, two cities — one under a state of siege relieved by a bloody ambush, the other threatened by an internal vendetta that is resolved as follows:

> A crowd, then, in a market place, and there
> two men at odds over satisfaction owed
> for a murder done: one claimed that all was paid,
> and publicly declared it; his opponent
> turned the reparation down, and both
> demanded a verdict from an arbiter
> as people clamored in support of each,
> and criers restrained the crowd. The town elders
> sat in a ring, on chairs of polished stone,
> the staves of clarion criers in their hands
> with which they sprang up, each to speak in turn,
> and in the middle were two golden measures
> to be awarded him whose argument
> would be the most straightforward.

(18.497-504)

Here are the fundamental elements of the Homeric games: the

sacred playground, the dispute, the mortal threat, the heralds as peacekeepers, the judge, the prize, the concept of justice, the equitable resolution of a potentially fatal disagreement. As Huizinga shrewdly remarks,

> The playful and the contending, lifted on to the plane of that sacred seriousness which every society demands for its justice, are still discernible to-day in all forms of judicial life. The pronouncement of justice takes place in a "court", for a start. This court is still, in the full sense of the word, the *hieros kuklos*, the sacred circle within which the judges are shown sitting, in the shield of Achilles. Every place from which justice is pronounced is a veritable *temenos*, a sacred spot cut off and hedged in from the "ordinary" world."[4]

Perhaps no episode in the *Aeneid* entails so extended and detailed a reworking of Homer as the Sicilian games with which Aeneas commemorates the anniversary of Anchises' death. Poised, like Homer's games, in a brief interlude between past losses and future triumphs, they, too, serve to recapitulate and assimilate the past as a necessary prelude to the future. While, from one point of view, the games in both epics are an escape from the struggles of daily life, from another, they can be seen to function as mirrors of the main actions of their respective poems. As shown above, however, the main thrust of the games for Patroclus is toward a reintegration of the schisms arising from the quarrel of Achilles and Agamemnon. While the Aeneadae are to some extent troubled by disunity, as the firing of the ships indicates, the thrust of the games for Anchises is predominantly toward the future. The culminating event of the Roman games, the *lusus Troiae* under the direction of young Iulus, with its extraordinary labyrinthine maneuvers, is the rite that will consecrate the founding of Alba Longa, the rite to be performed annually by Julius and Augustus Caesar. *Fatum* (destiny), which everywhere pervades and shapes the *Aeneid*

and orients it so strongly toward the future, has no counterpart in the *Iliad*, just as the *Iliad* has no counterpart to the
rite of the *lusus Troiae*. Although the fall of Troy is foreseen,
the future after that is a blank. Virgil's preoccupation with a
historical destiny for the Roman people, a destiny largely
accomplished at the time of his writing, gives to his games a
fundamentally different character from those of Homer. To
begin with, the games are conditioned by and subordinated to
this national future. They are rehearsals, preludes "to the
swelling act of the imperial theme." This is apparent not only in
the *lusus Troiae* but in the opening event of the ship race, which
is modeled on Homer's chariot race and which is also, like
Homer's chariot race, the longest and the most significant
contest in the series.

The historical context of Virgil's ship race imposes a
collective ideal entirely absent from the individualistic emphasis
of Homer's chariot race. Virgil's contestants are triremes, whose
success or failure depends not only on the captains, but on the
gubernatores at the helms, as well as on the unnamed toilers
at the triple banks of oars below, who provide a powerful
lesson in the unquestioning obedience that the great Roman ship
of state requires of its citizens. Even the worth of a captain is
determined by the extent to which he adheres to the collective
political ideal. A reckless pursuit of victory at all costs, in which
the ship of Sergestus is disabled, is as reprehensible as the
excessive caution of the aged helmsman Menetes or the rash
anger of his captain, Gyas. Avoiding *timor* on the one hand and
furor on the other, the vessel of Cloanthus takes first place. And
why does Cloanthus win? Because in addition to seamanship
and good judgment, he showed *pietas* in praying to the gods of
the deep and vowing rich sacrifices to them. Bands of Nereids,
Phorcus, and Panopea hear his prayers, and father Portunus
drives him on his way (5.238-42).

As Michael Putnam observes, "the theme of victory by

sacrifice, of achievement gained only through death, which in the games always ends in the comic relief of narrow personal escape, is the focal idea of the rest of the contests."[5] While this is also true of the Homeric games, "the various episodes of the first race suggest a comic microcosm of the final stretches of Aeneas' journey which embraces the loss of pilot, narrow escape from shipwreck, and final safe arrival at a destination."[6] This symbolism bordering on allegory, and absent from Homer, seems to derive from the historical foreshadowing that shapes Virgil's poem.

Virgil's ship race is a game of a special sort. Like the four other events, it is a war game. The utility of these maneuvers for the impending conquest of Italy is obvious. The element of play and the spirit of holiday, which have comparatively free reign in Homer, are subordinated in Virgil to the demands of an imperial destiny, just as Waterloo once dominated the playing fields of Eton. Thus the élan and spontaneity that mark Homer's games are greatly diminished in Virgil. Menetes' and Sergestus's discomfiture evokes collective laughter from the assembled troops in which one detects a hectoring note. History and destiny have conditioned the Trojan refugees in a way unknown to Homer's Achaians, and the resulting subordination of the games to military and political ends has impaired their purity. Roger Caillois affirms six essential characteristics of games: they must be free, separate, uncertain, unproductive, regulated, and fictive.[7] Virgil's ship race satisfies these requirements only in part. For one thing, the contending ships are not volunteered but explicitly chosen from the whole fleet. For another, the contest is so closely related to battle maneuvers that it cannot be called separate. And while it does seem to satisfy the criterion of uncertainty, its purpose in conditioning the crews for battle scarcely qualifies it as unproductive. Finally, while it is regulated, its utility as battle training makes it more realistic than fictive. In contrast to the Homeric games, which exemplify to a high degree Caillois's play principle, Virgil's seem to be work in disguise. If we accept Caillois's opposition between the world of play and the world of reality, Virgil's games fail to meet the test, since "every contamination [of the world of games] with ordinary life runs the risk of corrupting and ruining its very nature."[8] This is not to suggest a failure in Virgil, but rather to point up the way in which the imperial theme transformed the character of heroic games by subordinating the individual to a collective ideal. To state the point more positively, Virgil modified the Homeric model of the chariot race in order to celebrate the qualities of teamwork, obedience, and temperance, collective virtues that stand in marked contrast to the more individualistic *areté* of the Homeric heroes.

Another contest that Virgil modeled on Homer is the footrace. But whereas in Homer, Ajax, the son of Oïleus, is leading when he slips on cow dung and falls, Virgil, introducing the same motif, elevates, in the interests of heroic decorum, the dung into the blood of a sacrificial animal. He further elevates the episode by introducing a romantic friendship between two of the contestants. This familiar episode, in which Nisus has the presence of mind to trip up Salius so that his young friend can win, is clearly another comic microcosm, this time anticipating Nisus's rash attempt to save Euryalus in an ambush in Book 9, an attempt that ends in tragedy. As Aeneas awards the prizes according to the order of finish, Salius makes a strenuous objection, a detail that Virgil adopts from the quarrel in Homer's chariot race. Aeneas's curious disposition of the case seems a striking miscarriage of justice (from *The Aeneid of Virgil,* trans. Allen Mandlebaum [New York: Bantam, 1972]):

> At this, the loud cries of Salius
> reach everyone within that vast arena:

the elders in the front rows and the crowd.
He asks that what was snatched from him by fraud
be given back. But popularity
protects Euryalus, together with
his graceful tears and worth that please the more
since they appear in such a handsome body.
The protests of Diores also help;
he then was nearing to receive his palm
and would have come in vain to claim third prize
if Salius were given back first honors.

(5.447-57)

Salius is awarded a splendid lion skin, whereat Nisus complains of his bad fortune and shows "his face and limbs befouled with wet filth" (5.472). "The best of fathers" appeases him with a fine shield.

If this episode is considered in the context of its Homeric counterpart, some interesting points emerge. Like Achilles, Aeneas sees to it that everyone gets a prize, but, unlike Achilles, he does not manage to have the dispute fairly arbitrated. Euryalus won only through Nisus's foul, but he retains first place. The distribution of prizes does not follow upon a fair determination of merit, but is partly a response to popular clamor and partly an act of appeasement. In Homer it is clear that Achilles is particularly fond of Antilochus, but he never allows this preference to override justice. When "the best of fathers" smiles on the cheat Nisus and awards him a prize, one senses an offensive note of paternalism in no way characteristic of Achilles. The whole affair is dishonorable, and Aeneas exhibits a patronizing imperturbability, which resembles that of Augustus Fagan, D.D.

In mimicking Virgil's imitation of Homer's games, Pope followed the Virgilian precedent of varying his models. Whereas Homer's main event takes place on land and Virgil's on the sea, the games of *The Dunciad* combine the elements in a sea of mud. Whereas Achilles and Aeneas, the presiding heroes, do not participate in any of the contests, Pope's new hero, Colley Cibber, sits immobilized upon his throne throughout the festivities, without acting or even speaking. The entire direction of the games is left to his goddess-mother, following the precedent, as Pope's argument tells us, of the games that Thetis proposes for her son, Achilles, in *Odyssey* 24. In contrast to the enthusiastic but orderly audience in Homer and Virgil, these games are thronged with a mob, a motley mixture of hacks and would-be noble authors.

The prizes for the first race are illusions beginning with the airy image of a poet for which booksellers are to contend. After loud heroic declamations, Bernard Lintot and Edmund Curll, whom Pope represents as venal and corrupt publishers, start racing. Like Ajax and Nisus, Curll slips and falls, losing first place to Lintot (from *The Dunciad in Four Books, The Poems of Alexander Pope*, ed. John Butt [New Haven, Conn.: Yale University Press, 1963]):

> Full in the middle way there stood a lake,
> Which Curll's Corinna chanc'd that morn to make:
> (Such was her wont, at early morn to drop
> Her evening cates before his neighbor's shop,)
> Here fortun'd Curll to slide; loud shout the band,
> And Bernard! Bernard! rings through all the Strand.
>
> (2.69-74)

Thus, in a clear elaboration of Homer and Virgil, Pope's hero comes a cropper on a pool of excrement that he is partly responsible for placing before his rival's shop. Unlike Ajax and Nisus, however, Curll, through the good offices of the minor chthonic nymph Cloacina, recovers from the fall and wins the race:

> Renew'd by ordure's sympathetic force,

As oil'd with magic juices for the course,
Vig'rous he rises; from the effluvia strong
Imbibes new life, and scours and stinks along;
Re-passes Lintot, vindicates the race,
Nor heeds the brown dishonors of his face.

(2.104-8)

Yet the phantom poet and the other prizes elude the victor's grasp and vanish. In this case the rewards are exactly commensurate with the merits of the contenders.

After contests in urinating, noisemaking, and tickling patrons, the games are moved to Fleet-ditch, a notorious sewer disemboguing on the Thames, "The king of dykes! than whom no sluice of mud/With deeper sable blots the silver flood" (2.273-74). The first event is mud throwing:

Here strip, my children! here at once leap in,
Here prove the best can dash through thick and thin,
And who the most in love of dirt excel,
Or dark dexterity of groping well.
Who flings most filth, and wide pollutes around
The stream, be his the Weekly Journals bound,
A pig of lead to him who dives the best;
A peck of coals a-piece shall glad the rest.

(2.275-82)

The mud-diving contest is won by the Archbishop of Canterbury, with the Bishop of London as runner-up. In all the Fleet-ditch sports the author, as Pope remarked, "tosses about his dung with an air of Majesty," and the indiscriminate enthusiasm of the contestants for these dirty doings achieves a perverse lyrical beauty in one diver's account:

First he relates, how sinking to the chin,
Smit with his mien, the mud-Nymphs sucked him in:
How young Lutetia, softer than the down,
Nigrina black, and Merdamante brown,

Vy'd for his love in jetty bow'rs below,
As Hylas fair was ravish'd long ago.

(2.331-36)

As I mentioned earlier, the cow dung that Ajax slips on in
Homer's race is a momentary intrusion of ordinary reality into
the purity and separateness of the play world, as is (though to
a lesser degree) the incident of Nisus's fall in Virgil. By making
mud and excrement the milieu of his games, instead of a brief
intrusion upon them, Pope seems to have inverted the relationship of the world of heroic games to the world of external
reality. His muddy and unworthy heroes and the games they
play with such zest inhabit a homogeneous and separate world
of heroic value. Unlike Waugh's games, which are vitiated by
a lack of rules and spatial or temporal limits, Pope's are
complete, regulated, and coherent *in terms of the standards
that inform them.*

An illuminating approach to the games of Dulness is
Emrys Jones's in his essay "Pope and Dulness." Noting that
Pope's heroes are infantile, Jones relates this detail to the
poem's central concern with words and with the Logos. If
the Dunces are arrested in a preverbal state, their activities
have the engaging and releasing appeal of child's play. He
also notes, along with Wilson Knight, the absence of cruelty
in these games:

Everyone is having a wonderful time, for within the imaginative world of the poem no one is conscious of humiliation.
These dunces are, in fact, like unabashed small children —
but children viewed with the distance and distaste of the
Augustan adult. The world they inhabit is, like that of early
infancy, wholly given to feeling and sensation, and so all the
activities are of a simple physical nature: they run races,
have urinating, tickling, shouting, and diving competitions,
and finally vie with each other in keeping awake until "the
soft gifts of Sleep conclude the day."[9]

The delight of the Dunces in "tossing the dung about with an air of Majesty" and in immersing themselves in it with such zest reflects the innocent anality of a very early stage in child development with a glance at the naiveté of "heroic" values. The reader realizes, of course, despite whatever delight he may feel in all this joyous excremental activity, that the dunces, like such infants, "cannot as yet truly act, since an act is based on the capacity for delay and choice and judgement." Instead of acting, they "impulse."[10]

The epic hero is a man of action, and his actions are judged by an agreed set of standards that can be expressed by one word—*honor*. Homer's games, for example, develop from a narrowly construed and egocentric concept of honor to one more extensive and humane. Since heroic action may include, under certain circumstances, the decision to refrain from certain actions, Antilochus's decision not to press his dubious victory over Menelaus at all costs is a form of heroic action. The later books of the *Odyssey* are filled with situations in which Odysseus is wronged, insulted, and tempted to impulsive acts of vengeance, acts that would momentarily gratify his rage and ultimately frustrate his victory over the suitors. Like Edgar in *King Lear*, he assumes "the basest and most poorest shape/That ever penury in contempt of man/Brought near to beast" (2.3.8). In order to encompass his true identity, he assumes for a while the rags and manner of a beggar—a No Man. His passiveness in the face of insult is, for the time being, a heroic virtue, and justified by the honorable goal at which he aims.

Clearly of a different order is the passivity of Pope's hero Cibber and of the dunces. Because they have no worthy or honorable goal, they are incapable of acting directly, just as they are incapable of refraining from hasty or dishonorable behavior, which is another kind of action. Such conduct is ultimately represented as a surrender of responsibility, an unselective reaction to their own impulses and external stimuli,

most richly exemplified in a vertiginous surrender to the downward pull of gravity. One critic has shrewdly observed that in
Paradise Lost to stand is to act, whereas to fall is recklessly
to fail to act.[11] The nadir of such passivity is reached in the
following passage from *The Dunciad*, Book 4:

> And now had Fame's posterior trumpet blown,
> And all the Nations summon'd to the Throne.
> The young, the old, who feel her inward sway,
> One instinct seizes, and transports away.
> None need a guide, by sure Attraction led,
> And strong impulsive gravity of Head:
> None want a place, for all their Centre found,
> Hung to the Goddess, and coher'd around.
> Not closer, orb in orb, conglob'd are seen
> The buzzing Bees about their dusky Queen.
> The gath'ring number, as it moves along,
> Involves a vast, involuntary throng,
> Who gently drawn, and struggling less and less,
> Roll in her Vortex, and her pow'r confess.
> Not those alone who passive own her laws,
> But who, weak rebels, more advance her cause.
>
> (4.72-86)

If the heroic games of Homer and Virgil ritualize the
integration of individuals within a context of moral and social
values, and the "un-games" of Waugh express the disintegration
of community values, Pope's antiheroic games mark a more
advanced stage in regression than one is likely to find anywhere
else in English literature. If individualism is rampant in Waugh's
games, it is nullified in Pope's. The underlying pattern of
Decline and Fall is circular. The book ends where it begins,
without a climax. The underlying pattern of *The Dunciad*,
mating the circle of futility with the downward pull of bathos,
is a vortex, and the climax is a nadir in which everything is
annihilated.

2

Gods at War

Like Gods they fight, nor dread a mortal Wound.
—Pope, *The Rape of the Lock*

If games can bring man closer to the divine, war may serve a corresponding function for the gods who are preoccupied with mortals, or for mortals who are quasi-divine. A prime example is the war between the sexes in *The Rape of the Lock*, which reaches a climax in an inconclusive battle between the partisans of Belinda, whose lock of hair has been cut, and the Baron, who has cut the lock and vows to keep it, despite the cries of Belinda's allies to "restore the lock." The contretemps is extensively modeled on the quarrel in *Iliad* 1 between Achilles and Agamemnon over the prize slave, Briseis. In Pope the crisis is not resolved. Belinda's appeals go unheeded, despite the efforts of her emissary, Sir Plume, which adumbrate the famous embassy to Achilles in *Iliad* 9. In a display of immovable resoluteness that recalls Achilles' oath in *Iliad* 1, the Baron declares:

But by this Lock, this sacred lock I swear,
(Which never more shall join its parted hair,
Which never more its Honours shall renew,
Clipt from the lovely Head where late it grew)
That while my Nostrils draw the vital Air,
This Hand, which won it, shall for ever wear.
He spoke, and speaking, in proud Triumph spread
The long-contended Honours of her Head.

(4.133-140)

Here Pope has ingeniously combined several Homeric motifs. The prized lock, which the intransigent Baron refuses to return despite the appeals of the assembled heroes, he also invokes as a sanction for his oath, in the manner of Achilles swearing on the scepter of Agamemnon. And just as Achilles stressed the irrevocable nature of his decision by reminding his audience that he was no more capable of going back on his oath than the scepter was of turning back into the tree from which it was cut, so the Baron stresses the irremediable nature of his act by reminding his audience that the lock can never again grow on Belinda's head. In the face of this irrefutable logic Belinda can only complain of what she regards as a violation of her honor, concluding her speech with the memorable couplet,

Oh hadst thou, Cruel! been content to seize
Hairs less in sight, or any Hairs but these!

(4.175-76)

Book 4 thus ends in a deadlock similar to the one in the *Iliad* involving Agamemnon, who has sworn to keep the prize taken from Achilles, and Achilles, who has sworn to withdraw from battle until the Achaeans suffer terrible losses without him.

In Book 5 Clarissa attempts to mediate the dispute in the manner of Nestor, but, unlike Nestor's even-handed speech, which finds faults on both sides, Clarissa's, however wise, is critical only of Belinda. Roused by the virago Thalestris, the

beaux and belles form parties and proceed to do battle. At
this point Pope compares the battle to certain theomachies in
the *Iliad* during which the various Olympians intervene on
behalf of their Achaian or Trojan favorites:

> No common weapons in their Hands are found,
> Like Gods they fight, nor dread a mortal Wound.
>
> (5.43-44)

In this drawing-room battle the warriors are not mere mortals
and protégés of the gods, but enjoy a quasi-divine status. The
distinction is all-important because it is the foundation of
Pope's mock-epic conception of this fashionable society, whose
denizens live in a world of Olympian detachment from the
pressures of time, decay, and other unpleasant realities
epitomized in "mortal wound." In the play world of Hampton
Court, though the godlike beaux and belles are immune to
mortal wounds, as are the Olympians, the overtones of the line
go far beyond this obvious point, as Pope develops the sexual
connotations of dying in the inconclusive battle that follows.
After invoking the theomachies during which

> 'Gainst *Pallas, Mars; Latona, Hermes* arms;
> And all *Olympus* rings with loud Alarms,
>
> (5.47-48)

Pope gives a curious twist to his parody. The godlike beaux
actually court death!

> While thro' the Press enrag'd *Thalestris* flies,
> And scatters Deaths around from both her Eyes,
> A *Beau* and *Witling* perish'd in the Throng,
> One dy'd in *Metaphor*, and one in *Song*.
> *O cruel Nymph! a living Death I bear,*
> Cry'd *Dapperwit*, and sunk beside his Chair.
> A mournful Glance Sir *Fopling* upward cast,

Those Eyes are made so killing—was his last.
Thus on *Meander's* flow'ry Margin lies
Th'expiring Swan, and as he sings he dies.

(5.57-66)

While the death these immortals suffer may be limited to word-play and metaphor, the Baron seeks a more substantial con-summation:

See fierce *Belinda* on the Baron flies,
with more than usual Lightning in her Eyes;
Nor fear'd the Chief th'unequal Fight to try,
Who sought no more than on his Foe to die.

(5.75-78)

This paradoxical love-death sought by the Baron suggests the only conceivable resolution of the dispute. For Belinda it is the only escape from an endless round of activities leading nowhere since, as Clarissa puts it, "She who scorns a Man must die a Maid."

The weapon with which Belinda now proceeds to attack the Baron ironically implies Clarissa's message and a great deal more:

Now meet thy Fate, incens'd Belinda cry'd
And drew a deadly *Bodkin* from her side.
(The same, his ancient Personage to deck,
Her great-great Grandsire wore about his Neck
In three *Seal-Rings*; which after melted down,
Form'd a vast *Buckle* for his Widow's gown:
Her infant Grandame's *Whistle* next it grew,
The *Bells* she gingled, and the *Whistle* blew;
Then in a *Bodkin* grac'd her Mother's Hairs,
Which long she wore, and now *Belinda* wears.)

(5.87-96)

Belinda's bodkin and the history of its metamorphoses carry

intimations of mortality, but intimations of marriage, birth, infancy, and old age as well. Everywhere in *The Rape of the Lock* the characters seem ageless, unchanging, eternally youthful. Their illusions of eternal youth allow them to play endlessly a mating game that never reaches a climax. Just as the Olympians, imprisoned in their immortality, are doomed to repetitive cycles of quarrels and feasts and inconclusive interventions in battle throughout most of the *Iliad*, Pope's belles and witlings are prevented by their unending cycles of treats, cards, balls, toilettes, and empty flirtations from escaping into life. The bodkin on which Belinda swears her irreconcilable oath is the comic counterpart of the scepter by which Achilles swears his irreconcilable hostility to Agamemnon, an oath fraught with catastrophic consequences. The scepter, as shown above, with its bloody and monstrous entail upon generation after generation, is an appropriate symbol of irredeemable tragedy. The bodkin is no such thing, but rather a symbol of the natural cycles of human life from birth to death. Were she to understand it aright, Belinda would see the bodkin as an emblem of her human destiny. The Baron is equally uncomprehending in the oath he swears by Belinda's ravished lock.

There are faults, then, on both sides, and whether it is Belinda, striving to recover the lock, or the Baron, determined to retain it, both are fighting over something that is not the true object of contention between them. The lock is obviously a polite surrogate for Belinda's maidenhood and for the Baron's un-satisfied masculinity. Were they both to fulfill their destinies, it would be her role to surrender to the Baron, after due rites of courtship and marriage, and the Baron's to cherish her, court her, and ease for her the transition from proud maiden to happy wife. The mating games with which they fill their days—the balls and treats and tea parties and rounds of cards—have lost their ritual functions and have turned into inconclusive frivolities. The lock, which can have only symbolic value, is misconstrued by both Belinda and the Baron as an object of great intrinsic value. In Pope's inspired use of the ancient ambiguity of the word *die* we find the real clue to a happy issue out of their existential *cul-de-sac*. Acceptance of mortality is a precondition to living fully. The fashionable round, as Pope puts it in a more somber mood in *Epistle to a Lady,* leads to a Dantesque circle in hell:

> See how the World its Veterans rewards!
> A Youth of frolicks, an old Age of Cards,
> Fair to no purpose, artful to no end,
> Young without Lovers, old without a Friend,
> A fop their Passion, but their Prize a Sot,
> Alive, ridiculous, and dead, forgot!
>
> (11.243-48)

Belinda's insistence on winning and her intransigent hostility to the Baron is clearly the Augustan mock-epic counterpart of the narrow notion of heroic honor that nourishes the quarrel between Agamemnon and Achilles. She would have done better had she, like Shakespeare's Juliet, looked upon love as a match to be won only by losing, a life to be won only by "dying":

> Come, civil night,
> Thou sober-suited matron, all in black,
> And learn me how to lose a winning match,
> Play'd for a pair of stainless maidenhoods.
>
> (3.2.10-13)

But since Belinda and the Baron remain irreconcilable on a point of false honor, the conflict remains a deadlock, climaxing in the Ovidian stellification of the lock.

The inconclusive melee of Pope's beaux and belles is an analogue to those equally inconclusive combats of the Olympians that occur at various points in the *Iliad*. What makes mortal combat significant, tragic, and conclusive—that is, mortality itself—cannot raise Homer's theomachies to a level of equal importance. For the Olympians war is play, and it is for this reason that the gods in the *Iliad* become figures of fun, as C.M. Bowra has remarked.[1] The battle of Pope's beaux and witlings is clearly founded on one of the most absurd of these theomachies, the battle-royal encouraged by Zeus in Book 21, a domestic farce in which Ares, trying to revenge himself on his sister, Athene, is laid low by a boulder from her ponderous hand, and Hera calls her daughter Artemis a "shameless hussy," boxes her ears, and scatters her arrows.

If the games for Patroclus mirror the serious concerns of the poem and provide a brief respite from them, in *The Rape of the Lock* the relation of games to serious concerns seems to be inverted. Where daily life is play, as in this hermetically sealed playground of Augustan society, what corresponds to the "reality" against which the confrontations of beaux and belles can be measured? There are a few pinholes in the otherwise impermeable membrane that encloses this timeless space, such as the intimations of mortality in Clarissa's speech, or in the oft-quoted line "Then wretches hang that jurymen may dine," or in the classic zeugmas juxtaposing the beau monde and the political world in:

Here *Britain's* Statesmen oft the Fall foredoom
Of Foreign Tyrants and of Nymphs at home;
Here Thou, Great *ANNA*! whom three Realms obey,
Dost sometimes Counsel take—and sometimes *Tea*.

(3.5-8)

Still, the fashionable life at this court is as exempt from the pressures of time and mortality as life on Olympus, with its round of drinking, squabbling, and intrigue. Having presented the ordinary life of beaux and belles *sub specie ludi*, Pope cast about, I believe, for an inner world that would reflect it, as the games in Homer reflect the ordinary world of

war, and he found it in the game of Ombre.² One aspect of
Pope's ingenious use of this game bears again on the important
distinction between play and ordinary reality. Where the normal
life of the court is inconsequential, the game of Ombre is
decisive: Belinda wins, and her victory precipitates the main
action of the poem. Moreover, the game seems more real and
its playing-card combatants more vital and human than the
etiolated youths who play the hands. The male court cards
assume a virile substantiality that Sir Plume, the Baron, and
the rest of the beaux and witlings have not, while the queens
are more truly feminine than the belles. In other words, sexual
differentiation is strongly marked:

> Behold, four *Kings* in *Majesty* rever'd,
> With hoary *Whiskers* and a forky *Beard*;
> And four fair *Queens* whose hands sustain a flow'r,
> Th'expressive *Emblem* of their softer Pow'r;
> Four *Knaves* in *Garbs* succinct, a trusty *Band*,
> *Caps* on their heads, and *Halberds* in their hand.
>
> (3.37-42)

Clearly a more rugged and simpler heroic world is evoked, in
which the passions and human attachments of the cardboard
images are deeper and stronger than those of the players, as
seen in the final, winning, trick:

> And now, (as oft in some distemper'd State)
> On one nice *Trick* depends the gen'ral Fate.
> An *Ace* of Hearts steps forth: The *King* unseen
> Lurk'd in her Hand, and mourn'd his captive *Queen*.
> He springs to Vengeance with an eager pace,
> And falls like Thunder on the prostrate *Ace*.
>
> (3.93-98)

Thus, Pope's delicious and unobtrusive irony has endowed the
royal cards, in the interlude of Ombre, with a solidity of

specification that outweighs their epicene manipulators. It is a play within a play that shows nature its own image.

When gods fight each other or fight with mortals, they may suffer pain, but immortality invariably renders the divine victim ludicrous. Immune to the irreversible consequences that mortals must endure, the gods of classical pantheons can only make of war what Milton calls "a civil game." Dr. Johnson's strictures on the war in Heaven in *Paradise Lost* 6 as a "confusion of spirit and matter"[3] have provided a useful departure for recent critical studies by Arnold Stein, Merritt Hughes, Joseph Summers, Stella Revard, and others.[4] For example, Stein's account of the war in Heaven as a "gigantic scherzo" takes one a long way toward appreciating an episode formerly regarded as a grotesque blot on the poem. Far from being an unintentional and tasteless farce in which not only the devils but the good angels are demeaned, the episode is defended as an expression of Milton's characteristic aversion to attempts to settle moral issues by force, while the discomfiture momentarily suffered by the loyal angels is both a challenge to Abdiel's somewhat facile assumption that

> When Reason hath to do with force, yet so
> Most Reason is that Reason overcome,
>
> (6.125-26)

and a test of their loyalty under pressure, "by humiliation and strong sufferance." I might add that Milton was drawing on theomachies in the *Iliad* to shape some of the key incidents in the war in Heaven and, above all, to set the tone for the central episodes in it.

As I remarked earlier, many absurd things happen in the *Iliad* when the gods intervene in mortal combat. In addition to the touches of domestic farce—Athene flattening her brother, who happens to be the god of war, with a rock, or Hera, when she grasps the wrists of her daughter Artemis, the huntress queen, with one hand, boxing her ears and scattering her arrows (as noted earlier) — there are some ludicrous encounters that, in spirit and in detail, lie behind certain key incidents in *Paradise Lost*. In *Iliad* 6 Diomedes, the *preux chevalier* of the Achaians during Achilles' absence, is incited by Athene to make forays against two of the gods. The first is Aphrodite, who, unwisely intervening on the Trojan side, has her hand pricked by the point of Diomedes' spear. With a shriek she flies up to Olympus and falls at the knees of her father Zeus to complain of what those nasty mortals have done. Zeus's response is a masterpiece of affectionate paternal irony: "Warfare is not for you, child. Lend yourself/to sighs of longing and the marriage bed. /Let Ares and Athena deal with war" (5.428-30). Comforted by her father and healed by the family doctor, Paieon, Aphrodite decides to keep apart henceforth from the struggle that is raging over her son, Aeneas. Apollo, however, now urges Ares to intervene on the Trojan side and avenge his sister. But the god of war is no more successful in the encounter than the goddess of love, as Diomedes, asisted by the formidable force of Athene, drives his spear deep into Ares' belly and pulls it out again.

> Then brazen Ares
> howled to heaven, terrible to hear
> as roaring from ten thousand men in battle
> when long battalions clash.
>
> (5.859-60)

Like his sister, the indignant Ares complains to his father, but this time Zeus's response is anything but consoling:

> "Do not come whining here, you two-faced brute,
> most hateful to me of all the Olympians.
> Combat and brawling are your element.

This beastly, incorrigible truculence
comes from your mother, Hera, whom I keep
but barely in my power, say what I will.
Still, I will not have you suffer longer.
I fathered you, after all;
your mother bore you as a son to me.
If you had been conceived by any other
and born so insolent, then long ago
your place would have been far below the gods."

With this he told Paieon to attend him,
and sprinkling anodyne upon his wound
Paieon undertook to treat and heal him
who was not born for death.

(5.888-901)

Untaught by this painful experience, Ares reenters the battle in Book 21, where, as shown above, he is laid low by Athene herself.

The two principal hand-to-hand engagements in the war in Heaven are modeled on Ares' encounters with Diomedes and Athene. In the first of these Michael wounds Satan grievously with his sword:

it met
the sword of *Satan* with steep force to smite
Descending, and in half cut sheer, nor stay'd,
But with swift wheel reverse, deep ent'ring shear'd
All his right side; then *Satan* first knew pain,
And writh'd him to and fro convolv'd; so sore
The griding sword with discontinuous wound
Pass'd through him, but th' Ethereal substance clos'd
Not long divisible, and from the gash
A stream of Nectareous humor issuing flow'd
Sanguine, such as Celestial Spirits may bleed,
And all his Armor stain'd erewhile so bright.
Forthwith on all sides to his aid was run
By angels many and strong, who interpos'd
Defense, while others bore him on their Shields

Back to his Chariot, where it stood retir'd
From off the files of war: there they him laid
Gnashing for anguish and despite and shame
To find himself not matchless, and his pride
Humbl'd by such rebuke, so far beneath
His confidence to equal God in power.
Yet soon he heal'd. . . .

(6.323-44)

For the first time in the poem Satan's apparent imperturbability is shattered, and, though he does not bellow like Ares, he "writhes to an fro convolv'd" and "gnashes for anguish and despite and shame." The wound is a deep one, yet Milton surprisingly draws on the account of Aphrodite's scratch to describe the "stream of Nectareous humor issuing [that] flow'd/ Sanguine." The corresponding detail in Homer is closely followed: "Now from the goddess that immortal fluid,/ ichor flow'd—the blood of blissful gods" (5.339-40). Milton's allusion here to the wounding of Aphrodite, the goddess who instigated the Trojan War, not only introduces a satirical sidelight on Satan's conduct, but underscores his responsibility for starting the war in Heaven. The analogues to the wounding of Ares, "most hateful to me of the Olympians," are manifold, detailed, and too obvious to enumerate.

An even richer example of Milton's adaptation of a mock-epic theomachy in Homer is the encounter between Abdiel and Satan. The first engagement, which begins the hostilities, is modeled on this purely mortal combat between Diomedes and Aeneas in the *Iliad*:

But Diomedes
bent for a stone and picked it up—a boulder
no two men now alive could lift, though he
could heft it easily. This mass he hurled
and struck Aineias on the hip, just where
the hipbone shifts in what they call the bone-cup,

crushing this joint with two adjacent tendons
under the skin ripped off by the rough stone.
Now the great Trojan, fallen on his knees,
put all his weight on one strong hand
and leaned against the earth: night veiled his eyes.

(5.308-18)

The Miltonic encounter leaves Satan confounded and in the
posture of the stunned Aeneas:

So saying, a noble stroke he lifted high,
Which hung not, but so swift with tempest fell
On the proud crest of *Satan*, that no sight,
Nor motion of swift thought, less could his Shield
Such ruin intercept: ten paces huge
He back recoil'd; the tenth on bended knee
His massy spear upstay'd. . . .

(6.189-95)

Abdiel's mighty blow, however discomfiting to Satan and his
cohorts (and all the more humiliating since it is struck by
one whom Satan condemns as a "seditious angel"), is necessarily
inconclusive, as is Michael's.

The third main hand-to-hand encounter is patterned on
the encounters of Ares in the *Iliad*. Between Gabriel and
Moloch, it climaxes the first day's battle, and the palm
goes to the good angels.

Meanwhile in other parts like deeds deserv'd
Memorial, where the might of *Gabriel* fought,
And with fierce ensigns pierc'd the deep array
Of Moloch furious King, who him defi'd,
And at his chariot wheel to drag him bound
Threaten'd, nor from the Holy One of Heaven
Refrain'd his tongue blasphemous; but anon
Down clov'n to the waist, with shatter'd Arms
And uncouth pain fled bellowing.

(6.354-62)

As Addison was one of the first to observe, Milton here "had his eye on Mars in the Iliad," adding that "The reader will easily observe how Milton has kept all the horror of this image without running into ridicule of it."[5] Yet the ridicule seems inescapable in view of Moloch's hyperbolical and blasphemous threats and, all the more so, in view of the close identification Milton has established between the most brutal of the rebel angels and Homer's most brutal god. Surely there is a comic discrepancy between Moloch here and Moloch as he conceives of himself in Book 2:

> His trust was with th'Eternal to be deem'd
> Equal in strength, and rather than be less
> Car'd not to be at all; with that care lost
> Went all his fear: of God, or Hell or worse
> He reck'd not. . . .

> (2.46-50)

Clearly Moloch's pose as Stoic hero is as shattered as his arms, and one cannot doubt that at the council of the rebel chiefs that ends this first catastrophic day of battle, he would have to agree with Nisroch's observation:

>   yet hard
> For Gods, and too unequal work we find
> Against unequal arms to fight in pain,
> Against unpain'd, impassive; from which evil
> Ruin must needs ensue; for what avails
> Valor or strength, though matchless, quell'd with pain
> Which all subdues, and makes remiss the hands
> Of Mightiest.

> (6.452-59)

The rebel angels, like Homer's combative Olympians, suffer pain, but unlike their Homeric counterparts, the devils learn from experience. To avenge their pain on their foes, and to defend themselves from any further hand-to-hand agonies, they resort to the secret weapon of cannon, invented, appropriately enough, by Satan. One should note that, according to the ancient Homeric code of heroic warfare, this is a gross violation of the rules of the game. None of the first-rate heroes in Homer employs a weapon that permits him to fight at a distance. Odysseus left his bow at home in Ithaca and never made use of the poisoned arrows that Mentes once brought him as a guest gift. True, bows are used in the Trojan war, but usually by heroes of dubious honor, like Pandarus and Paris. The unwritten protocol seems to be that a first-rate hero should only fight with a weapon that puts him in immediate range of his adversary. This point is underscored by the fact that a tentative truce between Trojans and Achaians, to permit a settlement of the war by a combat between chosen champions, is breached by Pandarus's wounding of Menelaus with an arrow. Not the least of the ironies surrounding Achilles' death, as anticipated in the *Iliad*, is that he dies from an arrow shot by Paris.

The huge concealed cannon employed by Satan's forces on the second day of the war in Heaven are simply a grosser violation of the rules of war. Against these unexpected weapons the loyal angels are helpless. The arch duplicity of Satan's puns is a marked departure from the forthright style in which contending heroes traditionally assert their claims to superior *areté*. (Not the least reprehensible product of the Satanic revolt is the labored and self-gratulating ambiguity of their comments on their astonished victims.) A comparison of the vitality that Pope's wordplay on "die" accumulates at the core of *The Rape of the Lock* points up the sterility and frivolity of Satan's puns, born, as Conrad Hyers suggests,[6] of deep despair. If, then, the labored *jeux de mots* of Satan and his cohorts strike the reader as stupid, they ought out to:

O Friends, why come not on these Victors proud?
Erewhile they fierce were coming, and when wee,
To entertain them fair with open front
And breast (what could we more?) propounded terms
Of composition, straight they chang'd their minds,
Flew off, and into strange vagaries fell,
As they would dance, yet for a dance they seem'd
Somewhat extravagant and wild, perhaps
For joy of offer'd peace: but I suppose
If our proposals once again were heard
We should compel them to a quick result.

(6.609-19)

Not the least of the sufferings that the good angels must now
endure are the scoffs of Satan's cowardly lieutenant, who dares
in this moment of absolute military superiority to ape his
master:

To whom thus *Belial* in like gamesome mood.
Leader, the terms we sent were terms of weight,
Of hard contents, and full of force urg'd home,
Such as we might perceive amus'd them all.
And stumbl'd many; who receives them right,
Had need from head to foot well understand;
Not understood, this gift they have besides,
They show us when our foes walk not upright.

(6.620-27)

The normal language of *Paradise Lost*, unexcelled in richness
and imaginative grasp, provides an instructive comment on these
devilish witticisms, which are characterized by imaginative
poverty. If true wit augments understanding with the powers
of reason and fancy, such false wit darkens understanding
through a deliberate perversion of the metaphorical process.
If wit enhances meaning, this systematic reductiveness is
antiwit, ultimately reduced to an infantile practical joke that
backfires. God's wit is true wit because it comprehends the

universal context in which Satan's machinations inevitably redound upon themselves.

The second day's fighting escalates the epic theomachy to its highest pitch. The loyal angels, whom the devils' artillery had bowled down like duckpins, cast aside weapons, shields, and armor and proceed to hurl enormous chunks of landscape at their foes. In this "jaculation dire," Milton carries the dialectic of immortal combat to its utmost conclusion, a deadlock that God sums up:

> sore hath been their fight
> As likeliest was when two such Foes met arm'd;
> For to themselves I left them, and thou know'st,
> Equal in thir Creation they were form'd,
> Save what sin hath impair'd, which yet hath wrought
> Insensibly, for I suspend their doom;
> Whence in perpetual fight they needs must last
> Endless, and no solution will be found:
> War wearied hath perform'd what War can do,
> And to disorder'd rage let loose the reins,
> With mountains as with Weapons arm'd, which makes
> Wild work in Heav'n, and dangerous to the main.
> Two days are therefore past, the third is thine;
> For thee I have ordain'd it, and thus far
> Have suffer'd, that the Glory may be thine
> Of ending this great War, since none but Thou
> Can end it.
>
> (6.687-703)

Critics of Milton's God have charged him with disingenuousness in permitting his loyal angels to fight a war he knows they can't win. While it is true that he seems to enjoy the spectacle somewhat like Zeus in *Iliad* 21, who "laugh'd in his heart for joy, seeing the gods/about to meet in strife" (389-90), and while his behavior may be defended on the grounds that he permits maximum freedom to men and angels alike, a more important reason for his allowing this indecisive theomachy to disturb the peace of Heaven for two days is that it provides a final and irrefutable demonstration of the futility of heroic warfare. Here is the ultimate example of that "tedious and fabled Havoc" Milton derides in the beginning of Book 9. Here is the ultimate criticism of the heroic code as narrowly conceived by some of its Homeric and Virgilian exemplars. Interestingly enough, in *Paradise Lost* not a single decisive act is achieved by force. Every deed of malevolent violence not only redounds upon the head of the doer, but is transmuted into good. Yet even in the hands of the virtuous, violence is ineffectual. The angelic squadrons who patrol the circuits of Eden with such vigilance, discipline, and panache are unable to prevent Satan's final incursion, and none of God's champions — Abdiel, Michael, or Gabriel — though armed with swords of ethereal temper, can win a decisive victory over Satan or any of his cohorts. The farce of the war in Heaven, in which irresistible forces collide with immovable bodies, produces a tremendous explosion in which the only serious casualty is the tradition of heroic warfare.[7] Only the Son can break the futile dialectic of violence entailed on the angelic armies by Satan, and the arms he uses are of the Spirit. "Exhausted, spiritless, afflicted, fall'n" (6.852), the rebel forces, after much belligerent posturing, nevertheless realize the hopelessness of force and, in their future undertakings, resort to fraud — a decision that deeply undercuts their pretensions to heroic virtue.

The war in Heaven, then, with its absurdity, farce, and bombastic hyperbole, is indeed a confusion of spirit and matter. The devils, "since by strength/They measure all, of other excellence/Not emulous" (6.820-22), attempt in their folly to defeat immortal spirits with the ponderous matter of their cannons (and the almost equally ponderous matter of their jokes). The good angels, partly under the false assumption that right is might, put their faith in arms that serve only to encumber and humiliate them. The gigantic scherzo purges this epic at its very center from the traditional epic fallacy of force. The poem is now free to move on to what Milton considers to be the only real arena of combat, one in which victory is won by "things deem'd weak/Subverting worldly strong and worldly wise/By simply meek" (12.567-69). For the victor who thus learns to lose a winning match, the arena will be transformed into the Paradise within.

3

Feast of Fools

Il est l'heure de s'enivrer! Pour n'être pas les
esclaves martyrisés du Temps, enivrez-vous; enivrez-
vous sans cesse! De vin, de poésie, ou de vertu,
à votre guise.

—Baudelaire, *Petits poèmes en prose*

Like games, feasts are set apart from normal quotidian
reality and allow room for a foolishness that would be inappro-
priate in ordinary life. In their pure state feasts of fools are
life-enhancing rituals that mock the myopic and monocular
vision that men sometimes must assume in transacting the world's
business. They convey the paradox that certain kinds of
spirited and enlightened folly are wiser than the wisdom of
worldlings. They derive, ultimately, from rituals that harmonize
the order of flesh with the order of grace. For Falstaff they
reconcile gravity and gravy. At the highest reaches of the feast
of fools one perceives—above even the sublime folly of Antony
and Cleopatra—the ultimate beatitude of Christ the Fool, which

78

lies at the imaginative center of Erasmus's great *Encomium moriae*.

Falstaff's comic metamorphoses in Shakespeare's *Henry IV* reflect and expose the affairs of the real world in much the same way that the games in the *Iliad*, the *Aeneid*, and *The Dunciad*, the fashionable pastimes of *The Rape of the Lock*, and the gigantic scherzo of Milton's war in Heaven reflect and comment on issues of consummate importance. Upbraided by his superior officers for tardiness in leading his tattered troops to the battlefield at Shrewsbury, Falstaff observes, in a famous aside, "Well, to the latter end of a fray and the beginning of a feast/Fits a dull fighter, and a keen guest" (4.2.80-81). This neat articulation of the ethics of survival provides a transition from the heroic code, which sets honor as the highest good, whether on the playing field, the field of battle, or the fashionable drawing-rooms of Augustan London, to a sort of Darwinian opportunism and adaptability by which Falstaff aggrandizes and nourishes himself under even the most unpromising circumstances.

Indeed, no mock-epic figure in literature has more keenly analyzed the limitations of the code of heroic honor than Falstaff. If, in his case, desire has so long outlived performance that his capacity to make love is on a par with his capacity to make war, time has in no wise impaired his appetite for sack and capons or his witty transcendence of the workaday world of unpleasing obligations and risks. Almost single-handedly Falstaff constructs a brilliant and delightful festive space with the qualified concurrence of the Prince and the half-witted cooperation of a notable collection of idiots, such as the Hostess, Bardolph, Poins, Peto, and those venerable Justices, Shallow and Silence. This festal world, which centers in the comic ghetto of Eastcheap, is more a state of mind than a physical place. The mobility that permits Falstaff to take it from the Boar's Head Tavern to the battlefield at

Shrewsbury and to Justice Shallow's estate in Gloucestershire helps to make it invulnerable to the forces of law and order bent on suppressing it. In its purest form, Falstaff's festive world is impervious to the reality principle, and it satisfies the theories of Huizinga and Caillois in being voluntary, separate, regulated, unproductive, uncertain, and fictive. Clearly the denizens of this world, the Prince included, are voluntary participants in fictive actions of a bewildering variety—plays extempore, homilies, mock battles, practical jokes, parodies, and even a robbery that is rendered fictive and unproductive (much to Falstaff's disgust) by the Prince's insistence on returning the loot. The principal game that Falstaff plays involves his putting himself in jeopardy and, at the last moment, when threatened with exposure as a coward or a liar or a cheat, through a tour de force of wit, catching his persecutors in the trap they have set for him. He uses folly as a stalking-horse to outwit his companions, and its most prevalent form is his assumption of a bewildering succession of roles that tease them into repeated and vain attempts to unmask him.

No element of the festive world of *Henry IV* links it more closely to the ordinary world of politics, the overriding concern of the *Henriad*, than the motif of Falstaff's counterfeiting, which parodies and exposes the hypocrisy of the counterfeit Henry IV and the self-deluding egotism of Hotspur. So long as he recognizes the fictive nature of his activities, Falstaff is secure. When he allows the imaginative license he enjoys in that world to encroach on the world of political power with the announcement (in Part 2) that "the laws of England are at my commandment" (5.3.138-39), he has destroyed his festive world. Whereas most games are corrupted by the intrusion of reality into their sacred space, Falstaff's games are corrupted by his besotted attempt to translate his dreams of unrestrained and lawless power into reality. At a crucial moment the irony and the sense of play that prevented him from making excessive demands upon the real world forsake him. It is not Hal who rejects Falstaff, in the long run, but Falstaff who engineers his own rejection and entraps himself.

All festive worlds focus on some aspect of timelessness. "Through the paradox of rite, profane time and duration are suspended."[1] The games Falstaff plays are designed to annihilate time, much as Belinda's "rites of pride" are vain rituals of eternal youth. According to Hugo Rahner, "To play is to. . .preempt the future, to give the lie to the inconvenient world of fact. In play earthly realities become, of a sudden, things of the transient moment, presently left behind, then disposed of and buried in the past."[2]

The innate opposition between time and the timelessness of the festive world is the fundamental ordering principle of the *Henriad* from which all other central issues branch. From Richard II's realization that he had indulged in empty rituals of divine right ("I wasted time, and now doth time waste me" — when the time was ripe for action) to Prince Hal's determination to redeem the time, as he does on the battlefields of England and France, these history plays explore the implications of that opposition with extraordinary imaginative and dramatic power. The historical theme running through the tetralogy endows the issue with epic importance. Not only are the civil wars and the crisis of succession to the throne of England as momentous as the Trojan War or the founding of the Roman empire, but Shakespeare went further than Homer in the *Iliad* and Virgil in the *Aeneid* by representing the consequences of civil disorder in the daily lives of ordinary subjects as well as in the lives of the great. In this respect one might claim that the *Henriad* outdoes its epic predecessors in scope by combining the high public concerns of the *Iliad* and the *Aeneid* with the humbler concerns of domestic life glimpsed in the *Odyssey*, familiar matter of today in the lives of herdsmen, small farmers, and slaves. The focus on time and history is thus a double one: now on the strategies of war and peace; now on the inconveniences of daily life brought on by civil disorder and wartime inflation.

In an opening speech (in Part 1) King Henry presents the country's plight from the first perspective, the view from the top, and the heroic verse reflects his point of view, while its validity is undercut when the reader realizes that the king knew what he was saying was untrue:

> So shaken as we are, so wan with care,
> Find we a time for frighted peace to pant
> And breathe short-winded accents of new broils
> To be commenced in stronds afar remote.
>
> (1.1.1-4)

The pious resolution to take England on a crusade turns out to be a bit of royal posturing when it is shown that the king already has news of another outbreak of civil war. Nonetheless, the lines, in their formal and figurative manner, convey a sense of England's distress. For a view from the bottom, consider this exchange between two carriers, which begins act 2 (Part 1):

> *Second Carrier.* Peas and beans are dank here as a dog, and that is the next way to give poor jades the bots. This house is turned upside down since Robin Ostler died.
> *First Carrier.* Poor fellow never joyed since the price of oats rose; it was the death of him.
> *Second Carrier.* I think this be the most villainous house in all London for fleas, I am stung like a tench.
> *First Carrier.* Like a tench? By the mass, there is ne'er a king christen could be better bit than I have been since the first cock.
> *Second Carrier.* Why, they will allow us ne'er a jordan and then we leak in your chimney, and your chamber-lye breeds flies like a loach.
>
> (2.1.1-22)

Thus, the *Henriad* (with the interesting exception of *Richard II*) is shot through with specific and evocative glimpses of the culture of the common man that counterpoint the heroic concerns of the court and the rebels. Often these homely glimpses of daily life express an authentic reality against which the political aspirations and strategies of royalty and nobility are shown to be spurious. Even more often, they establish a rhythm of ordinary life firmly based on a prospering agriculture that the designs and machinations of the great may sometimes disturb but never destroy. Just as the similes in the battle scenes of the *Iliad* often represent some familiar moments in the life of country-folk—a farmer opening up an irrigation ditch; a woodsman putting aside his ax after a hard morning's work; a mother brushing flies away from her nursing child; a boy building a sandcastle by the sea—the representations of country life in the *Henriad* provide a norm that comments tacitly on the events of the epic. Sometimes bordering on festivity, as in the senile and bibulous hospitality that Justice Shallow offers Falstaff in Gloucestershire, these glimpses of country life, taken altogether, constitute an immemorial natural cycle of seedtime and harvest that is distinguished, on the one hand, from the linear drive of history, and, on the other, from the timeless moment of festivity.

At their best, the Eastcheap follies draw their material from the low world of ordinary life and the high world of war and politics, and transmute it by the power of Falstaff's comic imagination into something that transcends both. The high world is vulnerable to parody because of its drastically narrow view of life, "a civilization that is perishing in the barren solemnity of a purely utilitarian view of life," as Rahner says of Hermann Hesse's *Magister Ludi (The Glass Bead Game).*[3] The low world is vulnerable because of its compulsive preoccupation with details, with getting and spending, and (most painfully) with collecting and paying debts. The separate claims of high world and low are neatly juxtaposed in the parallel terms *death* and *debt*, pronounced alike, the force of both claims being brought home emphatically to Falstaff at Shrewsbury when Hal reminds him that "he owes God a death" (5.1.126). Hal's remark precipitates the famous soliloquy by which Falstaff reduces honor to "a mere scutcheon": " 'Tis not due yet: I would be loath to pay him before his day. What need I be forward with him that calls not on me" (5.1.127-28). Death and debt (aggravated by Falstaff's chronic "consumption of the purse") are the forms in which time presses most threateningly upon Falstaff's festive world. The Hostess, to whom he owes money, can be fobbed off by promises of marriage and other subterfuges. His strategies against the fell sergeant are more complex, including repeated vows to mend his ways, pretenses that he is young ("they hate us youth"), and attempts at outwitting death by impersonating it on the battlefield.

In a milder and more pervasive form, the pressure of time on Falstaff's world appears as appetite, which must be appeased by Gargantuan quantities of sack and capons. Being, like any true parasite, constitutionally indisposed to work, he must live by his wits. Necessity mothers the inventions by which he nourishes his belly, and the inventions are almost always theft in some form or other, the only "vocation" Falstaff is willing to "labor in."

The theme of thievery so pervasive in the subplot reflects, of course, the doings of both the high and the low worlds of *Henry IV*. The crown that the King has stolen is plotted for by a group of rebels who fall out through petty squabbles. Hotspur, "the theme of honor's tongue," claiming a third of the kingdom to which he has not the shadow of a title, makes matters worse by picayune intransigence in the division, "cavilling over the ninth part of a hair" (3.1.138), thus alienating some of his allies. While the great are carving up old England, the low are plundering on a smaller scale, although to the utmost of their capacities. In Gadshill's words, he and his fellow brigands "pray continually to their saint, the commonwealth, or rather, not pray to her, but prey on her, for they ride up and down on her and make her their boots" (2.1.82-85). This chilling speech has the mirthless ambiguity of Satan's puns in the war in Heaven. It cannot help but qualify our inclination to see Falstaff's role at the Gadshill robbery as a bit of harmless horseplay.

Beneath the hilarity of Falstaff's Eastcheap follies there lies a more sinister intent to gain wealth and power through influencing the Prince. His festivities repeatedly threaten to spill over the walls of the playground and drown the surrounding countryside. This would have happened at Gadshill but for the intervention of the Prince. It almost happens at Shrewsbury, in the heat of battle, when the Prince borrows Falstaff's pistol, only to find it is a bottle of sack. The Prince cries, "What, is it a time to jest and dally now?" (5.3.55). The question goes to the heart of the nature of Falstaff's play. As his career progresses, his play becomes less and less characterized by that separateness from the world of reality that Huizinga and Caillois stipulate as the *sine qua non* of true games. Whether he indulges in such unseasonable acts of buffoonery or the greedy delusions that let him think the laws of England are at his commandment, Falstaff in the long run is a player who violates the necessary limits without which true play and true festivity cannot exist.

To move back now into the main argument, let us consider an episode that does function brilliantly as a comic microcosm of the great world, the play extempore that Falstaff proposes on the grounds that Hal should prepare himself for what promises to be a difficult session with his father on the morrow:

Well, thou wilt be horribly chid tomorrow

when thou comest to thy father;
If thou love me, practice an answer.

(2.4.373-75)

Falstaff seizes the opportunity to mimic the aloof solemnity of King Henry in ponderous moral truisms couched in equally ponderous euphuistic rhetoric, in the meantime praising himself as the one virtuous man among the Prince's companions. The psychological strategies Falstaff is covertly employing are described by Ernst Kris in his "Psychology of Caricature," as follows:

> The primary social character of tendentious forms of comic expression appears to be conditioned by two factors. In the first place, another person's approval is used to justify one's aggression. And furthermore, wit and caricature can easily be recognized as an invitation to that other person to adopt a joint policy of aggression and regression.[4]

The playfulness of the episode, enhanced by Falstaff's foolish and apparently harmless impersonation, is actually a covert expression of *lèse-majesté*. In his caricature (in Part 1) of Henry as sententious, pompous, and insensitive, he is undermining the authority of the royal father and attempting to disarm the strictures he anticipates on himself:

> There is a thing, Harry, which thou has often heard of and it is known to many in our land by the name of pitch. This pitch, as ancient writers do report, doth defile; so doth the company thou keepest: for, Harry, now I do not speak to thee in drink but in tears, not in pleasure but in passion, not in words only, but in woes also; and yet there is a virtuous man whom I have often noted in thy company, but I know not his name.

(2.4.453ff.)

The comic absurdity of the play extempore does not entirely conceal Falstaff's strategy, as an Aristotelian *bomolochos*, of disguising his aggressive buffonery against the King as affectionate concern for Hal. His caricature of Henry as an *agroikos*, a humorless boor, is strengthened by the fact that the King really is humorless and utterly lacking in that Aristotelian virtue of *eutrapelia* that lies midway between buffoonery and boorishness.[5] "The tendentious forms of comic expression" Falstaff employs, aided by the King's unapproachable and uncomprehending nature, "assist the conquest and seduction of the partner."[6] Suddenly, however, Hal "deposes" Falstaff, assumes the role of royal father, and proceeds to anathematize Falstaff in comic hyperboles that do not wholly conceal his underlying determination someday to break with him. To the sentimental plea — "but for sweet Jack Falstaff, kind Jack Falstaff, true Jack Falstaff, valiant Jack Falstaff, and therefore more valiant being, as he is, old Jack Falstaff, banish not him thy Harry's company, banish not him thy Harry's company, banish plump Jack, and banish all the world!" — the Prince tersely replies, "I do, I will" (2.4.475ff.).

The Prince thus blocks Falstaff's tendentious plea, assumes the role of royal responsibility, and, in a way Falstaff never intended, uses the play extempore to prepare himself for tomorrow's talk with his father. The comic exhilaration that the reader feels in watching this scene can hardly be attributed to the intrinsic wit or to the subtlety or brilliance of the impersonations. The fact that the witless Hostess is overcome by the virtuosity of the acting should be sufficient critical comment on this point. The essential interest of the scene lies elsewhere, in the fact that behind the buffoonery of the play extempore Falstaff is playing a different game for high stakes, and Hal knows it. On the outcome of that game, at the end of Part 2, depends the future of the kingdom.

As C. L. Barber has shown, the Prince's "sense of timing. . . , the relation of holiday to everyday and doomsday" make him the real exemplar of the spirit of play.[7] It is he who exemplifies that *eutrapelia* which strikes the proper balance between gravity and festivity. It is he who realizes that there can be no holidays without working days:

If all the year were playing holidays
To sport would be as tedious as to work;
But when they seldom come, they wished-for come,
And nothing pleaseth but rare accidents.
So, when this loose behavior I throw off
And pay the debt I never promised,
By how much better than my word I am,
By so much shall I falsify men's hopes;
And, like bright metal on a sullen ground,
My reformation, glitt'ring o'er my fault,
Shall show more goodly and attract more eyes
Than that which hath no foil to set it off.
I'll so offend to make offense a skill,
Redeeming time when men think least I will.

(1.2.209-21)

While conceding an unpleasantly calculating element in the Prince's character, I believe that he avoids Hotspur's obsessive and vain pursuit of honor, which leaves him one of the fools of Time, and Falstaff's subversive denigration of honor, which, at the end of Part 2, makes him another. As Walter Kaiser says,

And so Falstaff, who has no concern for time, is unable to perform that redemption of the time that St. Paul calls for in his Epistle to the Ephesians; he is an Ephesian of the old, not the new church. It is the prince, not his Epicurean companion, who, aware that they are playing 'fools with the time' (2:II.ii.154), will perform the role of redeeming time when men think least he will.[8]

The rejection of Falstaff, Barber argues, marks a "drastic restriction of awareness which goes with the embracing of magical modes of thought, not humorously but sentimentally."[9] While one cannot deny that Hal's awareness appears to be restricted, the occasion has to a large extent been forced upon him by Falstaff, and he can hardly stop the coronation procession to deliver an apologia. The public occasion and the critical national obligations he has now assumed require the rejection of private indulgences and the repression of disorderly impulses, but not, perhaps, his self-righteous tone. While his lines, "redefining his holiday with Falstaff as a dream, and then despising the dream, seek to invalidate that holiday pole of life, instead of including it,"[10] Falstaff, at the end of Part 2, is no longer a delightful holiday figure but a real threat, a thief and a scofflaw who is plotting revenge on the Lord Chief Justice. The sentimentality is his, also, as he confuses self-serving motives with true affection. Magic is the illusion that the will, with the aid of certain words and gestures, can accomplish its desires. While the leading practitioner of this vain art in the *Henriad* is Richard II, Falstaff comes in a close second.

The career of Falstaff moves from a creative and life-enhancing folly that thwarts the deadly monocular vision of Henry IV and Hotspur, to the destructive folly that masks insatiable greed. His attempt to extend his regime beyond the limits of play forces a confrontation with law and authority that leads inevitably to his rejection. In his last words to Falstaff the new king simultaneously implies his role as God's vicegerent and identifies his old comrade as a "profane. . .fool and jester" (5.5.52-54). Part of the reader's discomfort with the speech is no doubt due to Hal's so suddenly invoking such religious sanctions. One can find here, nevertheless, submerged hints about a destructive "comic profanation of the sacred" against which the kingdom must defend itself.

Religious profanation of the sacred is obviously minimal in the *Henriad*, yet it is at the thematic center of the *Odyssey*. The comrades of Odysseus who ate the sacred oxen of the Sun are condemned in the very beginning of the poem as guilty of sinful folly, and the same unequivocal condemnation is pronounced by Zeus in respect to the murder of Agamemnon. These lines that Milton quotes at the crux of his discussion of obedience and free will in *Christian Doctrine* (Book 1, chapter 4) are also the model for the central dogmatic statement on the same subject made by God in *Paradise Lost*, as He anticipates man's transgression "of the sole command,/Sole pledge of his obedience" (3.94-95) in eating the fruit of the Tree of Knowledge. The threat of divine punishment for violation of such taboos also hangs over the uproarious suitors of Penelope, who violate the laws of gods and men by endlessly feasting uninvited in Odysseus's hall.

It has been observed that Homer's heroes spend much time in feasting. Normally these feasts are accompanied by ritual sacrifices to the gods, thus fulfilling Josef Pieper's observation, noted earlier, that without the gods there are no feasts.[11] Such customary rites of piety are often accompanied by rites of hospitality, especially in the *Odyssey*, where the constant voyaging of the heroes makes hospitality a matter of survival and a solemn obligation of the host. The Homeric feast is thus an important religious and social occasion, marked by abundant food, wine, and entertainment, generally consisting of epic narratives sung to the accompaniment of a harp by an *aoidos*, who enjoys a place of honor. These leisurely interludes also provide opportunities for strangers to entertain their hosts and fellow guests with tales of their own adventures. Since the events of Troy loom large over the entire *Odyssey*, the poem is filled with tales both true and false of adventures on the way back from the Troad.

The model feast in Homer takes place in Phaiacia, where

Odysseus has the good fortune to land after numerous trials and misadventures that have left him alone, exhausted, and without resources. The Phaiacians are a virtuous and hospitable folk, and, after a suitable interval, Odysseus regales them with the entire story of his adventures in the ten years since the fall of Troy, a story that consumes four Books and keeps the Phaiacian court up far past their usual bedtimes. So impressed are they with the distinction of their guest that King Alcinous levies a general assessment on his nobles to provide the departing Odysseus with suitable gifts. The importance of the occasion is further celebrated with special games and entertainments, the climax of which is the story of how Hephaistos trapped his adulterous wife, Aphrodite, with Ares, to the vast amusement of the other gods. This is sung to the harp of Demodokos and accompanied by dance (from *The Odyssey*, trans. Robert Fitzgerald [New York: Doubleday, 1961]):

> At the serene king's word, a squire ran
> to bring the polished harp out of the palace,
> and place was given to nine referees —
> peers of the realm, masters of ceremony —
> who cleared a space and smoothed a dancing floor.
> The squire brought down, and gave Demodokos,
> the clear-toned harp; and centering on the minstrel
> magical young dancers formed a circle
> with a light beat, and stamp of feet. Beholding,
> Odysseus marvelled at the flashing ring.
>
> Now to his harp the blinded minstrel sang
> of Ares' dalliance with Aphrodite:
> how hidden in Hephaistos' house they played
> at love together, and the gifts of Ares,
> dishonoring Hephaistos' bed — and how
> the word that wounds the heart came to the master
> from Helios, who had seen the two embrace;
> and when he learned it, Lord Hephaistos went
> with baleful calculation to his forge.

There mightily he armed his anvil block
and hammered out a chain, whose tempered links
could not be sprung or bent; he meant that they should hold.
Those shackles fashioned, hot in wrath Hephaistos
climbed to the bower and the bed of love,
pooled all his net of chain around the bed posts
and swung it from the rafters overhead —
light as a cobweb even gods in bliss
could not perceive, so wonderful his cunning.
Seeing his bed now made a snare, he feigned
a journey to the trim stronghold of Lemnos,
the dearest of earth's towns to him. And Ares?
Ah, golden Ares' watch had its reward
when he beheld the great smith leaving home.
How promptly to the famous door he came,
intent on pleasure with sweet Kythereia!
She, who had left her father's side but now,
sat in her chamber when her lover entered;
and tenderly he pressed her hand and said:

"Come and lie down, my darling, and be happy!
Hephaistos is no longer here, but gone
to see his grunting Sintian friends on Lemnos."

(8.257ff.)

Although moralistic critics from Plato on have been disturbed
by the open adultery and flippant attitude of some of the
gods toward it, the *Odyssey's* most recent editor finds the
episode charming and points out that the moral is good since
the offenders are punished.[12] In any event, the episode is much
in the spirit of the *hieros gamos* of *Iliad* 14, where Hera
seduces Zeus, an episode of high comedy during which the king
of the gods makes a fool of himself.

Within the context of the Phaiacian court, a model of
culture, hospitality, and piety, the Olympian bedroom farce
that crowns the elaborate festivities may seem a discordant
note. On the other hand, if one follows the argument of
Conrad Hyers, whose chief example is the medieval Feast of

Fools, this episode may be a legitimate instance of "the comic profanation of the sacred," which he describes as follows:

> Humor as a profanation of the sacred, however, is to be differentiated from that which has no basis in the sacred, from that which is not grounded in faith. Religious expression functions within a delicate dialectic between faith and laughter. On the one side is the peril of idolatry; on the other side is the peril of cynicism. Faith without laughter leads to dogmatism, while laughter without faith leads to despair.[13]

The tale of Ares and Aphrodite and Hephaistos is a burlesque of the central motif of the *Odyssey*, marriage. It is sung on the eve of Odysseus's return home after a twenty-year absence. The motif of marriage is not only the hero's uppermost concern, but one marked by the exemplary relationship of his host and hostess, King Alcinous and Queen Arete, and their nubile daughter, Nausicaa, who succors the shipwrecked Odysseus. With these thoughts in mind Odysseus says to her:

> And may the gods accomplish your desire:
> a home, a husband, and harmonious
> converse with him — the best thing in the world
> being a strong house held in serenity
> where man and wife agree. Woe to their enemies,
> joy to their friends! But all this they know best.
>
> (6.182-87)

Unlike the *Iliad*, where the gods, as advocates of Achaians or Trojans, are continually at odds, the *Odyssey* shows a remarkable harmony among the Olympians, beginning with their agreement (in the absence of Poseidon) to help the much-enduring Odysseus to reach his home. The postwar stability of Olympus underscores the pervasive ethical emphasis of the *Odyssey*, where the newly established moral order is never successfully challenged. As in the High Middle Ages, when faith could tolerate the comic profanation of the sacred, the postwar era, after the defeat of Troy and the return of Helen to Menelaus, could celebrate its new security with the charming and instructive *fabliau* involving the deities of war and desire. In view of Odysseus's imminent return to Ithaca and Nausicaa's impending marriage, the bedroom farce on Olympus can be read as a fertility rite in which sexual passion is regulated by the bonds of marriage.

The *Odyssey*, that quintessential romance of marriage, anticipated innumerable romantic comedies, such as *Twelfth Night, As You Like It,* and *The Tempest*. At the center of most is a feast of fools that mocks established social and moral values, even while renewing and endorsing them. In the *Odyssey* the antithesis of the beneficent Phaiacian follies is the unending and turbulent feast in which Penelope's suitors indulge during the absence of Odysseus. This, too, is a feast of fools, but one marked by contempt for all the values that are celebrated in the other. Devouring the substance of Odysseus, insulting his queen, plotting the murder of his son, ignoring sacrifices to the gods, these cynics violate all the conditions that define a true feast. The climax of their profanities occurs when Odysseus, disguised as a beggar soliciting their alms, is rewarded with a cow's hoof flung by Ktessippos, an outrage which, among others, brings about a bloody nemesis.

Phaiacian political and social institutions, then, are strong enough to tolerate and even benefit from an interlude of festive folly, while Ithaca is threatened with chaos by the unbridled turbulence of the suitors. The truly well-ordered society permits the maximum freedom to its members. This is especially true when its values have won wide allegiance, as in the *Odyssey*. Unlike the *Iliad*, where even the gods are disputing fundamental issues, the *Odyssey* presents a world in which the prevailing values are never in doubt.

Another work of Shakespeare's in which personal and public values are hopelessly at odds, is *Antony and Cleopatra*. In some ways closer in fact and spirit to the chaotic brawlings of Penelope's suitors than to the harmony of the Phaiacian festivities are the feasting and folly that constitute the play's lifeblood. Where they are absent, the atmosphere is dry and humdrum, as in the workaday world of international politics, whose center is Rome. The dull austerities of Roman life are such that next to politics the chief preoccupation in the imperial city is the goings-on in Alexandria. In Rome, where everything is done by the rule, the excesses of Egypt exert the kind of fascination that those of Paris once had for small-town American veterans of the First World War. Even the censorious speech of a Roman officer on the first entrance of Antony carries an undertone of awe:

> Nay, but this dotage of our general's
> O'erflows the measure. Those his goodly eyes,
> That o'er the files and musters of the war
> Have glow'd like plated Mars, now bend, now turn
> The office and devotion of their view
> Upon a tawny front; his captain's heart,
> which in the scuffles of great fights hath burst
> The buckles on his breast, reneges all temper,
> And is become the bellows and the fan
> To cool a gipsy's lust.
>
> (1.1.1-10)

Philo is unquestionably right: Antony *is* overdoing it in turning from his role as "the triple pillar of the world. . .into a strumpet's fool."[14] In response to Cleopatra's provocations he declaims:

> Let Rome in Tiber melt, and the wide arch
> Of the rang'd empire fall! Here is my space.
> Kingdoms are clay; our dungy earth alike

Feeds beast as man; the nobleness of life
Is to do thus, when such a mutual pair

[Embracing]

and such a twain can do't. . . .

(1.1.33-38)

Here, as in *Henry IV*, the fundamental conflict lies between
a world of festive excess and a world of public responsibility,
whose values are mutually critical. The world of public
responsibility, centered in Rome, is even more deeply corrupted
by hypocrisy, dissension, and murderous infidelities than that
of *Henry IV*, and the festive life of Alexandria is equally
corrupted by sensuality, treachery, and self-indulgence. Com-
pared to the Alexandrian follies, those in Eastcheap seem like
a Sunday-school picnic, and Antony has no such justification
as Hal's for thereby seeking valuable insights into human nature.
Antony already knows too much. Thus Shakespeare has nicely
poised his contending worlds, and, after jumping from one pan
of the scale to the other several times, Antony goes down with
Cleopatra, who has been equally adroit in shifting her
allegiances.

The issues are thus much more equivocal and evenly
balanced than they are in *Henry IV*, in which Hal has a
clearly recognized obligation to support the throne and preserve
it for himself. The claims of all the aspirants to power in
Antony and Cleopatra are clouded. The name of the game is
realpolitik, and Antony decides that it's not worth playing.
Once he has made his move back to Cleopatra, however, he
finds at first that she's not worth having. The result is a
fascinating dilemma that is still being hotly debated.

If there appears to be little to choose between Rome
and Alexandria, Shakespeare has nevertheless imbued both
places with contrary symbolic and atmospheric values. Rome is
"a civilization that is perishing in the barren solemnity of a
purely utilitarian view of life," as Conrad Hyers said of the

"idiotic earnestness" that Hesse exposes in *Magister Ludi*.[15] The Roman vision is compulsively focused on power, to which every other value is sacrificed, as in the cynical match that Octavius arranges between his sister Octavia and Antony. The relationship is repeatedly referred to in terms of unslipping knots and hoops. And as Caesar's farewell adjurations to his new brother-in-law show, the Roman idiom is characteristically materialistic and pedestrian:

> Most noble Antony,
> Let not the piece of virtue which is set
> Betwixt us as the cement of our love,
> To keep it builded, be the ram to batter
> The fortress of it.
>
> (3.3.27-31)

Antony, who casually marries Octavia for his "peace," while acknowledging to himself that his pleasure lies "in the east," is fluent in this Roman idiom of squares, rules, measures, and knots, as his farewell remarks, uttered a few moments earlier, indicate:

> My Octavia,
> Read not my blemishes in the world's report.
> I have not kept my square; but that to come
> Shall all be done by th'rule.
>
> (2.5.4-7)

It is hard to tell whether Antony is utterly unprincipled or simply absentminded. He is, at any rate, very impressionable, which one cannot say of Octavius.

The Egyptian idiom is in every way the opposite of the Roman devotion to limits, measures, and heavy materials like stone, concrete, and earth. Constantly challenging limits, the Alexandrian vision's characteristic modes are hyperbole and paradox. To the typical Roman the closest thing to paradox is contradiction. Something either is or is not, hence Philo's slow wonder that the triple pillar of the world could become a strumpet's fool, as well as Caesar's simplistic contrast between Antony the hedonist and Antony the Stoic (or perhaps more properly, the masochist):

> Antony,
> Leave thy lascivious wassails. When thou once
> Was beaten from Modena, where thou slew'st
> Hirtius and Pansa, consuls, at thy heel
> Did famine follow; whom thou fought'st against
> Though daintily brought up, with patience more
> Than savages could suffer. Thou didst drink
> The stale of horses and the gilded puddle
> Which beasts would cough at. . . .
>
> (1.4.55-63)

The Romans pride themselves on their realism, on their firm and efficient political and military action. They like the land and prefer to let the Egyptians and Phoenicians go a-ducking. This strong proclivity for material solidity is attended by an over-riding preoccupation with formalities and proprieties in personal relations. When Caesar first sees Octavia after Antony has allegedly abandoned her, his chief concern is that she has come unattended by a large train:

> Why have you stolen upon us thus? You come not
> Like Caesar's sister. The wife of Antony
> Should have an army for an usher, and
> The neighs of horse to tell of her approach
> Long ere she did appear; the trees by th'way
> Should have borne men, and expectation fainted,
> Longing for what it had not; nay, the dust
> Should have ascended to the roof of heaven
> Rais'd by your populous troops. But you are come
> A market maid to Rome, and have prevented

The ostentation of our love, which, left unshown,
Is often left unlov'd.

(3.6.42-53)

Thus the Roman world is hard, solid, public, dry, formal, limited.

"Roman wisdom consists in confining oneself to the possible; but Egyptian wisdom always dares more than what it can. Antony may be a strumpet's fool (I.i.13) but Octavius is after all only fortune's knave (V.ii.3)."[16] This shrewd observation in Janet Adelman's *The Common Liar: An Essay on "Antony and Cleopatra"* points the way to the ultimate distinction between Roman and Alexandrian values, otherwise so evenly balanced. The worldly wisdom of Caesar is ultimately doomed and leaves him at the end of the play "an ass unpolici'd" (5.11.310), while the folly of Antony and Cleopatra can be transcendent. This capacity for transcendence in its fertility and excess is reflected in the physical world of Egypt: its earth is mingled with water, its slime "quickened" by the sun's fire. Whereas Rome appears to be made of one element, earth, all the elements combine to produce the vital atmosphere of Egypt. Antony's opening allusion to "the dungy earth," and the numerous references with which the play is inwoven to the function of organic decomposition in the proliferation of Egypt's teeming life, point to the inseparable interdependence of corruption and vitality. Shakespeare explores the implication of this natural paradox in tracing the complex relationship between his aging lovers. That they are corrupt is beyond question. The real issue is whether or not this corruption breeds something of value. Cleopatra at least affirms this when she says, "I am fire and air; my other elements/I give to baser life" (5.2.292-93).

Nothing presents the Roman-Egyptian contrast more vividly than the succession of feasts described, represented,

or mentioned in the course of the play. Our initial impression
of an Alexandrian feast is highly unfavorable and biased,
despite Octavius's claim that he is being fair:

> You may see, Lepidus, and henceforth know,
> It is not Caesar's natural vice to hate
> Our great competitor. From Alexandria
> This is the news: he fishes, drinks and wastes
> The lamps of night in revel; is not more manlike
> Than Cleopatra, nor the queen of Ptolemy
> More womanly than he; hardly gave audience, or
> Vouchsaf'd to think he had partners. You shall find there
> A man who is the abstract of all faults
> That all men follow.
>
> (1.4.1-9)

After Lepidus's feeble defense of Antony, a defense in which
the faint praise is damning indeed, Caesar continues his indict-
ment of Antony in words whose constricted sounds wonderfully
convey his exquisitely offended fastidiousness:

> You are too indulgent. Let's grant it is not
> Amiss to tumble on the bed of Ptolemy;
> To give a kingdom for a mirth; to sit
> And keep the turn of tippling with a slave;
> To reel the streets at noon, and stand the buffet
> With knaves that smell of sweat: say this becomes him, —
> As his composure must be rare indeed
> Whom these things cannot blemish, — yet must Antony
> No way excuse his foils, when we do bear
> So great weight in his lightness.
>
> (1.4.16-25)

Among the other limits Rome maintains is a strict caste
system that would sniff at the kind of camaraderie that
obtains between Antony and his comrades-in-arms. After Antony
returns with his troops from the victorious second battle, he
says to Cleopatra:

Had our great palace the capacity
To camp this host, we all would sup together
And drink carouses to the next day's fate,
Which promises royal peril. Trumpeters,
With brazen din blast you the city's ear;
Make mingle with our rattling tabourines,
That heaven and earth may strike their sounds together,
Applauding our approach.

(4.8.32-39)

Antony's generosity of spirit on such an occasion (and even in defeat) is in vivid contrast to Caesar's aloofness and meanness of spirit as he anticipates victory:

Let our best heads
Know that tomorrow the last of many battles
We mean to fight. Within our files there are,
Of those that serv'd Mark Antony but late,
Enough to fetch him in. See it done,
And feast the army; we have store to do't,
And they have earn'd the waste.

(4.4.10-16)

What can the psychologists tell us of the inner life of a commander who sees "feast" only as "waste," and who conceives of his festal function as limited to directing a subordinate to convey his order through channels to the quartermaster who will duly issue extra rations? I see *Antony and Cleopatra* as Shakespeare's most probingly satirical play. Unlike *Henry IV*, from which few characters emerge without looking foolish, there is no figure in *Antony and Cleopatra* who is not in one way or another a fool. The biggest fools of all, however, are those superefficient war wagers whose perspective on reality is what Blake called the single vision and Newton's sleep.[17] Better that the fool persist in his folly, which in this play is the only possible path to any sort of wisdom.

If Caesar fails to catch the true spirit of festivity, his

fellow triumvirs aboard Pompey's yacht take part in what must
be the closest thing that ancient Rome could provide to a
fraternity initiation. As the party "ripens to an Alexandrian
feast" (as Antony puts it), Enobarbus arranges a rondeau of
the four world-sharers, who "make battery to our ears" with
this song:

> Come thou monarch of the vine,
> Plumpy Bacchus with pink eyne!
> In thy fats our cares be drown'd,
> With thy grapes our hairs be crown'd!
> Cup us till the world go round,
> Cup us till the world go round!
>
> (2.7.120-25)

As Caesar says, "What would you more?" This stag debauch,
in which Pompey, Lepidus, Caesar, and Antony are celebrating
their new amity, is shadowed by Menas's suggestion to Pompey
that, by slitting the throats of his three partners, he might
become lord of all the world. Pompey, in a fit of what the
disgusted Menas regards as scrupulosity, refuses the offer with the
remarkable observation:

> Ah, this thou should'st have done,
> And not have spoke on't. In me 'tis villany;
> In thee 't had been good service. Thou must know,
> 'Tis not my profit that does lead mine honour;
> Mine honour, it. Repent that e'er thy tongue
> Hath so betray'd thine act. Being done unknown,
> I should have found it afterwards well done
> But must condemn it now. Desist and drink.
>
> (2.7.79-86)

Pompey's speech is in the spirit of Bolingbroke's words in
Richard II to Sir Piers Exton, who actually performed the act
Menas had suggested:

Exton. From your mouth, my lord, did I take this deed.
Boling. They love not poison that do poison need,
Nor do I thee. Though I did wish him dead,
I hate the murderer, love him murdered.
The guilt of conscience take thou for thy labor,
And neither my good word nor princely favor.

(5.6.37-42)

Though treachery is rife in Egyptian political circles, and for a while Cleopatra entertains the idea of turning to Caesar to preserve Egypt, it is not directed as a rule to the ruthless pursuit of political power. Roman *realpolitik* is unequivocally exposed as the dialectic of unrestrained political ambition to which all other considerations are sacrificed.

No such judgment can be passed on the Egyptian world. "It is the unique excellence of *Antony and Cleopatra*," according to Adelman, "that it does not allow us to maintain the comfortable and certain attitudes of either comedy or tragedy for very long. We are not permitted the luxury of total engagement with the protagonists; nor are we permitted the emotional safety of total detachment from them."[18]

If the play confounds our judgment by a kaleidoscopic succession of contradictory or ambiguous images of the lovers, it leaves us with a vision, to whatever extent created out of their illusions, that excess may lead to the palace of wisdom, or something like it, not to be attained by the pseudostoicism of Rome. In subjugating personal values to pragmatic political ends Rome becomes a mockery of any valid social or political order. As Caesar's message to Cleopatra shows, "the time of universal peace" entails her putting herself under the "shroud" of "the universal landlord" (3.13.71-72). His is the order of the graveyard. Against his deadly tyranny any resistance tends to assume the most extreme forms of revolt or folly.

While they both reject the deadly values Caesar represents, Antony and Cleopatra, in a final paradox, transcend the

ambiguities of their lives by invoking Roman honor at their
deaths: Antony, "a Roman by a Roman valiantly vanquished"
(4.15.57-58), and Cleopatra a suicide "after the high Roman
fashion" (4.15.87). Excess and limit are thus reconciled.

But there is a further paradox. The high Roman fashion is
neither that of Aeneas nor certainly that of Octavius, the
Augustus for whom Virgil wrote his Roman epic, but that of
Cleopatra's prototype, Dido. Indeed, Shakespeare has rewritten
the major personal episode of the *Aeneid* to celebrate the
loving suicidal folly of Dido, which is endorsed by Antony's
words:

> Where souls do couch on flowers, we'll hand in hand,
> And with our sprightly port make the ghosts gaze:
> Dido and her Aeneas shall want troops,
> And all the haunt be ours.
>
> (4.14.51-54)

Shakespeare, "by imagining the two united in Elysium. . .makes
of their affair not a dangerous interlude which Aeneas skillfully
overpassed, but rather a resting place more final than Rome
itself. Dido and *her* Aeneas: the very type of a heroic resistance
to love has become the type of lover for Antony."[19] The
Odyssean bedroom farce of Aphrodite and Ares has been
transmuted into a triumphant heroic mockery of Roman *gravitas*
and Egyptian self-indulgence. The festival of love that *these*
fools have celebrated achieves a timeless validity through their
deaths.

Humanum est errare

Underlying the wise folly and the foolish wisdom at the
center of *Henry IV* and *Antony and Cleopatra* is a philosophical
paradox that has been traced back to "Alcibiades' contradictory,

paradoxical description of Socrates in the *Symposium*":[20]

> For fyrst it is not unknowen, how all humaine thynges lyke
> the *Silenes or double images of Alcibiades*, have two faces
> much unlike and dissemblable, that what outwardly seemed
> death, yet lokyng within ye shulde fynde it lyfe: and on the
> other side what seemed life, to be death; what fayre to be
> foule: what rich, beggerly: what cunnyng, rude: what
> stronge, feable: what noble, vile: what gladsome, sadde:
> what happie, unlucky: what friendly, unfriendly: what
> healthsome, noysome. Briefly the Silene ones beyng undone
> and disclosed, ye shall fynde all thynges tourned into new
> semblance.[21]

This is the famous speech of Folly that lies at the heart of her
paradoxical encomium upon herself. Yet unlike many other of
the paradoxes of Erasmus's *Encomium moriae*, it ultimately
leads to at least a limited resolution of what seem like
mutually exclusive attitudes to folly, of which there are two
kinds: the unredeemable calculation of self-interest (what
Shakespeare calls "Commodity" in *King John*), and the ability
at crucial times to abandon exclusive reliance on the evidence
of reason, to make the leap into faith, to say with Tertullian,
Credo quia impossibile est.

As seen above, *Antony and Cleopatra* teems with conflicting
assessments of the chief characters. Cleopatra, anguished over
Antony's marriage to Octavia, sees him as a contradictory
figure somewhat like Alcibiades' Socrates: "Though he be
painted one way like a Gorgon,/The other way 's a Mars"
(2.5.116-18). Antony, in turn, anguished by evidence that
Cleopatra has "packed cards with Caesar," reminds her that he
found her "as a morsel, cold upon/Dead Caesar's trencher:
nay. . .a fragment of Gnaeus Pompey's" (3.13.116-18); at other
times his "Egyptian dish" is more appealing, as in the words
of Enobarbus:

Other women cloy
The appetites they feed, but she makes hungry
Where most she satisfies; for vilest things
Become themselves in her, that the holy priests
Bless her when she is riggish.

(2.2.235-39)

The most Erasmian aspect of this speech is the assertion that "vilest things become themselves in her," which can mean either that in her the vilest things are somehow becoming, or that in her the vilest things fulfill themselves. The second meaning would clearly include the pervasive association in the "Alexandrian" values of the play of slime and corruption as the indispensable medium for fertility and beauty. In any event, what is "vilest" in Cleopatra is inseparable from what is "rarest." The two aspects are related to each other like the two faces of the Silenus-like Socrates as described by Erasmus's Folly. "Vilest things," then, become a part of what Rosalie Colie refers to as "negative theology," in which "rhopographical images" (insignificant objects) and "rhypological images" (sordid objects) become a way of approaching a metaphysical mystery,[22] in this case, the infinite variety of Cleopatra.

There can be little doubt that Shakespeare has created an ironical mock-encomium in a dramatic form that has profound affinities with Erasmus's *Encomium moriae*. The protean variety of Folly has its counterpart in the wealth of conflicting impressions one has of Cleopatra, the resolution of which depends not so much on a final assessment and judgment of the evidence as on one's imaginative surrender to paradox. In both situations judgment is confounded not only by contradictory and ambiguous evidence but, more importantly, by the self-referential worlds of Folly and of Antony and Cleopatra. Ultimately the *Encomium moriae* goes a step beyond the transcendence that the lovers claim for themselves by the subtle process through which Folly escapes for a time from solipsistic self-reference. The ultimate folly she celebrates, that of the fool in Christ, has the metaphysical underpinnings of Christian paradox that are not available to Antony and Cleopatra.

> In spite of her skepticism of scriptural interpretation, she herself cites and explicates passage after passage from Ecclesiastes and Paul's Epistles. . .in order to praise holy foolishness and therefore, herself. In her own representation, the classical Epicurean figure changes into the Pauline fool of God: Socrates' self-comment, that his only knowledge was that he knew nothing, becomes Folly's Christian comment upon her own nature. The Silenus-box does turn inside out to reveal Saint Socrates praying for us. In Erasmus' classical world there is a Christian sanctuary.[23]

While it would seem to be true that Folly undergoes some sort of dialectical development, as Richard Sylvester has argued,[24] it is important to remember, as Colie goes on to remind her readers, that the *Encomium moriae* does not end with the vision of the Fool in Christ:

> But even this observation, paradoxical though it is, is too direct a statement for paradox to permit; Folly does not fail us in her final self-contradiction and self-denial. Mocking her audience for its efforts to follow her radically disrupted and distracting discourse, Folly takes her equivocal farewell [I abstract from passage quoted]:
>
> "I perceive ye loke for an *Epiloge* or knotte of my tale, but than sure ye are verie fooles, if ye wene that I yet remember what I have spoken, after such a rablement of wordes powred forth. . . .Fare ye well therefore, clappe your hands in token of gladnesse, live carelesse, and drinke all out, ye the trusty servantes and solemne ministers of Folie."[25]

Yet, though this festive and trifling foolery stops (rather than ends) the *Encomium*, there shines above it the remembrance of praise of folly that is truly sublime:

> A most inhuman and economical thing, and more to be
> execrated, that those great princes of the Church and true
> lights of the world should be reduced to a staff and a
> wallet. Whereas now, if there be anything that requires their
> pains, they leave that to Peter and Paul, that have leisure
> enough; but if there be anything of honor or pleasure, they
> take that to themselves. By which means it is, yet by my
> courtesy, that scarce any kind of men live more voluptuously
> or with less trouble; as believing that Christ will be well
> enough pleased if in their mystical and almost mimical pon-
> tificality, ceremonies, titles of holiness and the like, and
> blessing and cursing, they play the parts of bishops. To work
> miracles is old and antiquated, and not in fashion now; to
> instruct the people, troublesome; to interpret the Scripture,
> pedantic; to pray, a sign one has little else to do; to shed
> tears, silly and womanish; to be poor, base; to be vanquished,
> dishonorable and little becoming to him that scarce admits
> even kings to kiss his slipper; and lastly, to die, uncouth; and
> to be stretched on a cross, infamous.[26]

Of the paradoxes implicit in Erasmus's title *Encomium moriae*
(*Folly's Praise of Folly*), Walter Kaiser remarks:

> As Erasmus's title thus doubles back on itself, it tends to
> cancel itself out in the fashion of a double negative. At
> least one is already tantalized by the doubt that it may
> cancel itself out. Or is it perhaps actually a triple negative?
> To begin to examine the problem is to condemn oneself
> to a vertiginous semantic labyrinth.[27]

As Kaiser attempts to follow out the logical implications of
Folly's self-praise, he demonstrates that reason is itself confounded in this labyrinth, from which the only escape can be
such a paradox as St. Paul's that "the foolishness of God is
wiser than men," and that "God hath chosen the foolish
things of the world to confound the wise."[28]

4

The Mazy Dance

Did ever he walk the twenty-six wards of the city, within
and extra, did he cast his nautic eye on her
                              clere and lusty under kell
in the troia'd lanes of the city?
                              — David Jones, *Anathémata*

From Homer to our own times the labyrinth has been a seminal
myth in art and literature. A central symbol in the *Aeneid*, as
Robert W. Cruttwell has shown,[1] is the Cretan labyrinth built
by Daedalus to enclose the monstrous Minotaur born to
Pasiphaë, the consort of King Minos. Athenian youths and
maidens were sacrificed periodically to the Minotaur until
Theseus, with the help of Minos's daughter, Ariadne, slew the
monster. The hero and the princess fled to Naxos, but the
architect and his son Icarus were imprisoned in turn and
contrived their escape with improvised wings. Icarus fell, of
course, and drowned in the sea to which he left his name,
having ignored his father's warning not to fly too high or too

close to the sun. Arriving in Sicily, Daedalus wrought a bas relief of the labyrinth that caught the eye of Aeneas as he was about to descend into the underworld. The episode is in *Aeneid* 6.[2] In a noteworthy book W. F. Jackson Knight has shown how mazes, labyrinths, and related spiral patterns surrounding cities, tombs, and various sacred places were believed to have an apotropaic and defensive character, as well as providing a ritual passage from the outer world to an inner place of spiritual illumination.[3] A contemporary Joycean, Jean Paris, has emphasized the significance of the labyrinth as a punitive enclosure.[4]

The most complete version of the Cretan myth is Virgil's, although Ovid gives the fullest treatment of Daedalus's flight from the labyrinth in *Metamorphoses* 8.[5] The Daedalian tablets that Aeneas ponders in *Aeneid* 6 foreshadow the extraordinary experience he is about to undergo. In his descent to the underworld Aeneas's mazelike movement will lead him through various terrors to a moment of illumination in which the ghost of Anchises shows him the future heroes of Rome.

In addition to the difficulties of penetrating to the center of the labyrinth or finding one's way out of it, Virgil adds another motif derived from Homer and elaborated — a labyrinthine dance in which the dancers reenact the movement toward and away from the center. This is the meaning of Homer's allusion to Ariadne's dancing floor and the dance depicted at the center of Achilles' shield in *Iliad* 18,[6] a dance that Virgil appears to imitate and elaborate in the cavalry maneuvers of the *lusus* (or *ludus*) *Troiae* — performed by Iulus and other youthful Trojans in *Aeneid* 5.[7] This ritual, Virgil tells us, will be reenacted at the consecration of Alba Longa, reinstated by Julius Caesar, and continued by Augustus. As Knight demonstrates, it is a ritual consecration of the city.[8]

The labyrinth and the mazy movements associated with it — Ariadne and her dancers or Iulus and his horsemen — is a central symbol of enormous complexity and power. While it can represent imprisonment and alienation, it also clearly represents penetration to a central place of mystical power and knowledge.[9] And while it represents bloody sacrifices, it can also represent the conquest of a murderous monster. Successful escape from what Virgil called its *inextricabilis* or *irremeabilis error*, celebrated in Ariadne's dance or the maneuvers of Iulus's cavalry,[10] also clearly represents an escape to freedom. Moreover, the imprisonment of Daedalus in his own maze can reflect the quandary of the artist, whose escape by the improvisation of wings suggests his transcendence of its limits through a more potent art. Thus the labyrinth subsumes a host of opposed possibilities: incarceration, death, sacrifice, and disorientation on the one hand; discovery, rebirth, sanctification, and deliverance on the other. In summing up its mythic potentials, C. R. Deedes has written:

> Above all, the Labyrinth was the centre of activities concerned with those greatest mysteries, Life and Death. There men tried by every means known to them to overcome death and to renew life. The Labyrinth protected and concealed the dead king-god in order that his life in the after-world might be preserved. There the living king-god went to renew and strengthen his own vitality by association with the immortal lives of his dead ancestors. The Labyrinth was the centre of the strongest emotions of the people — joy, fear, and grief were given the most intense forms of expression. These emotions were directed into certain channels, producing ritual and the earliest forms of art — not only music and dancing, but also sculpture and painting. The Labyrinth, as tomb and temple, fostered the development of all art and literature, activities which in those days possessed a religious and life-giving significance.[11]

Western man's oldest pictorial art, the cave paintings at Lascaux and elsewhere in southern Europe, demonstrates the

truth of this statement. As G. R. Levy shows, those Cro-
Magnon artists depicted in the deepest recesses of their
caves not only the game they hunted and lived on but the
terrifying bears and lions that also occupied the caves.[12] It
was from such living encounters of Cro-Magnon man with the
predatory animals with whom he shared the dark recesses of
these caverns that the myth of the anthropophagous Minotaur
in its labyrinth appears to have arisen. The extremely dangerous
and difficult approaches, as Levy also shows, with their vestiges
of human and animal footprints still visible, are traces of our
ancient ancestors' initiatory rituals. Thus the descent under-
ground to a place of terror and mystery as a *rite de passage*
was first enacted long before Aeneas could have made his
descent to Avernus.

Many are the ways in which the successors of Homer,
Virgil, and Ovid have employed the motifs of the maze and
associated patterns of labyrinthine or spiral descent or ascent.
If, for example, the completed movement to the center and away
from it can be schematized as a double cone, with the downward
penetration represented by one cone and the upward escape by
another, the resulting pattern is not only at the center of
Aeneas's experiences in the *Aeneid* (Books 6 and 7), but it
also supplies the structural pattern of the *Divine Comedy*. The
downward spiral is the necessary ordeal that provides the novice
with the knowledge and strength to complete the upward
spiral. While the pattern is also present in *Paradise Lost*,
it is not a pervasive structural principle as in Dante, but a
symbol Milton uses intermittently, most prominently in the case
of Satan's voyage from Hell to Earth.

The mock-epic emphasis of *MacFlecknoe* and *The Dunciad*
requires a radical modification of the completed pattern. For
the vertiginous or precipitate descent there is no corresponding
ascent. Dryden's and Pope's dunces may aspire to "soar above

th'Aonian Mount," but they are skilled only in the art of sinking. Father Flecknoe's final abrupt descent drops him "yet declaiming" through the trapdoor of what, in theatrical terms, was conventionally known as Hell. All that ascends is the bard's mantle, which will remain to invest the new Prince of Dulness.

In Pope's more elaborately Virgilian and Miltonic mock epic, lateral motion is added to the irresistible power of gravity, so that there is a pervasive downward-spiraling movement, especially in Books 3 and 4, in addition to futile labyrinthine movements. In the somber climax it is not the patrons of Dulness who descend but her enemy, the Word.

The Dunciad seems to be disposed around Books 5 and 6 of the *Aeneid*. As shown above, the games in Book 2 are closely modeled on the games in *Aeneid* 5, while Cibber's most adventurous experience in the whole poem is the Aeneas-like descent into an underworld of Dulness in Book 3, a descent characterized, however, by passivity and inertia, without a trace of Virgilian tension. The facility of Cibber's passage and his inertness in the underworld define satirically the torpid and effortless character of the Dunces' literary productions. Pope has devised a suggestive and pervasive image for these qualities in combining the bewildering features of the maze with the unresisted downward force of gravity. The result is a downward-spiraling vortex whose point may represent a number of themes, including the annihilation of reason. Pope's downward gyre of bathos shows the attractive power of egotism, unlike Yeats's upward spiral, which leads to chaos because "the center cannot hold."

Pope's central conception of "dulness" as the offspring of pride, and of pride as a kind of rampant self-assertion that, paradoxically, leads to the obliteration of the self, finds its proper image in this downward-moving vortex. Against the heroic and legitimate aspirations of Milton's muse to "soar above th'Aonian Mount," he presents his Dunces as whirling downward to a "no-place" of darkness and annihilation.

One first encounters the labyrinth motif in Book 1, where Dulness pays a royal visit to Grubstreet, a "Chaos dark and deep,/Where nameless Somethings in their causes sleep" (55-56). In this place of confusion — half Hell, half Garden of Adonis — she finds varied examples of literary formlessness and nonsense:

> [Here] hints, like spawn, scarce quick in embryo lie
> [Here] new-born nonsense first is taught to cry,
> Maggots half-formed in rhyme exactly meet,
> And learn to crawl upon poetic feet.
> Here one poor word an hundred clenches makes,
> And ductile dulness new meanders takes;
> There motley images her fancy strike,
> Figures ill-pair'd, and Similes unlike.
> She sees a Mob of Metaphors advance,
> Pleas'd with the madness of the mazy dance. . . .
>
> (1.59-68)

This pageant of the amorphous, with its strangely precise but meaningless activities subsumed in "meanders" and "the mazy dance," finds its counterpart in Cibber's abortive struggle to write:

> Swearing and supperless the Hero sate,
> Blasphem'd his Gods, the Dice, and damn'd his Fate.
> Then gnaw'd his pen, then dash'd it on the ground,
> Sinking from thought to thought, a vast profound!
> Plung'd for his sense, but found no bottom there,
> Yet wrote and flounder'd on, in mere despair.
> Round him much Embryo, much Abortion lay,
> Much future Ode, and abdicated Play;
> Nonsense precipitate, like running Lead,
> That slip'd thro' Cracks and Zig-zags of the head;
> All that on Folly Frenzy could beget,
> Fruits of dull Heat, and Sooterkins of Wit.
>
> (1.115-26)

The passage is obviously indebted to Satan's Chaotic voyage in *Paradise Lost* 2, with its formless and confused conflict of "embryon atoms." Cibber, "plunging for his sense," is a modified and antiheroic Satan bent upon a downward quest:

> At last his Sail-broad Vans
> He spreads for flight, and in the surging smoke
> Uplifted spurns the ground, thence many a league
> As in a cloudy Chair ascending rides
> Audacious, but that seat soon failing, meets
> a vast vacuity: all unawares
> Flutt'ring his pennons vain plumb down he drops
> Ten thousand fadom deep. . . .
>
> (2.927-23)

Pope thus joins Satan's vertiginous ascent from Hell to suggestions of the descent to the underworld, a motif he makes explicit in Book 3. He also carries over into his poem the Miltonic suggestion that for Satan the way up and the way down are the same:

> Which way I fly is Hell; myself am Hell;
> And in the lowest deep a lower deep
> Still threat'ning to devour me opens wide,
> To which the Hell I suffer seems a Heav'n.
>
> (4.76-79)

For the Prince of Dunces Dulness, like Hell for the Prince of Devils, is a state of mind. The labyrinth in which Cibber is lost is in his head.

In his sacrifice to Dulness Cibber's elaborate offerings of unreadable and unsellable books ("Redeem'd from tapers and defrauded pies") are topped off with a neat little Baroque motif of aspiration:

> An hecatomb of pure, unsully'd lays

> That altar crowns: A folio Common-place
> Founds the whole pile, of all his works the base:
> Quartos, octavos, shape the less'ning pyre;
> A twisted Birth-day Ode completes the spire.
>
> (1.158-62)

This upward thrust is offset by the oblique and ponderous movements of a Dunce's mind:

> O thou! of Bus'ness the directing soul!
> To this our head like byass to the bowl,
> Which, as more pond'rous, made its aim more true,
> Obliquely wadling to the mark in view:
> O! ever gracious to perplex'd mankind,
> Still spread a healing mist before the mind;
> And lest we err by Wit's wild dancing light,
> Secure us kindly in our native night.
> Or, if to Wit a coxcomb make pretence,
> Guard the sure barrier between that and Sense;
> Or quite unravel all the reas'ning thread,
> And hang some curious cobweb in its stead!
>
> (1.169-80)

Into these thwart obliquities Pope has woven Shadwell's pseudo-Jonsonian humoresque (from *MacFlecknoe*), "Obliquely wandering to the end in View"; crossed it with another telling echo from Dryden ("Thy chase had a Beast in View"); and added an allusion to the protective mists that Venus from time to time throws about Aeneas, permitting him to see unseen (although here they prevent the hero from seeing). The brilliant *cento* culminates in images of the mazy dance: rather than "err by Wit's wild dancing light," Cibber implores his goddess-mother to "quite unravel all the reas'ning thread,/And hang some curious cobweb in its stead!" The goddess responds by extinguishing the scarcely combustible materials of Cibber's sacrifice with a sheet from Ambrose Philips's uncompleted poem. *Thule:*

Sudden she flies, and whelms it o'er the pyre;
Down sink the flames, and with a hiss expire.

(259-60)

In Book 2 of *The Dunciad* Pope extends the motifs of sinking and falling to include a host of individual Dunces, most notably in the Fleet-ditch diving contests discussed earlier, and concludes the games with a reading from the "pond'rous books" of contemporary authors that stupefies the audience:

Who sate the nearest, by the words o'ercome,
Slept first; the distant nodded to the hum.
Then down are roll'd the books; stretch'd o'er 'em lies
Each gentle clerk, and mutt'ring seals his eyes.
As what a Dutchman plumps into the lakes,
One circle first, and then a second makes;
What Dulness dropt among her sons imprest
Like motion from one circle to the rest;
So from the mid-most the nutation spreads
Round and more round, o'er all the sea of heads.

(2.401-10)

While the lesser Dunces sleep, overcome by the contagious force of dull books, the goddess proceeds in Book 3 to initiate her protégé into the *mysterium tremendum* of her arts. In the opening scene, "in her Temple's last recess inclos'd," she combines, vis à vis her son Cibber, the role of the Sibyl in presiding over Aeneas's *rites de passage* with the protective (though sometimes obfuscating) maternal role of Venus. In this descent to the underworld's dusky vale there is, of course, no trace of Aeneas's strenuous ordeal: "And now, on Fancy's easy wing convey'd/The King descending, views th'Elyzian shade" (13-14). Cibber is actually asleep.

Elkanah Settle, in the role of Ascanius, now reveals the metempsychotic wonders of this pseudo-Virgilian underworld to his unconscious heir:

"Oh born to see what none can see awake!
Behold the wonders of th'oblivious Lake.
Thou, yet unborn, hast touch'd this sacred shore;
The hand of Bavius drench'd thee o'er and o'er.
But blind to former as to future fate,
What mortal knows his pre-existent state?
Who knows how long thy transmigrating soul
Might from Boeotian to Boeotian roll?
How many Dutchmen she vouchsaf'd to thrid?
How many stages thro' old Monks she rid?
And all who since, in mild benighted days,
Mix'd the Owl's ivy with the Poet's bays?
As man's Maeanders to the vital spring
Roll all their tides, then back their circles bring;
Or whirligigs, twirl'd round by skilful swain,
Suck the thread in, then yield it out again:
All nonsense thus, of old or modern date,
Shall in thee centre, from thee circulate."

(3.43-60)

The mystery of reincarnation in Virgil, through which past and future are linked, is here collapsed into a timeless and meaningless cycle in which the soul of the archdunce obliviously "thrids" and unthrids a labyrinthine chain of obtuse identities. Pope has subtly introduced Ariadne's guiding thread, which led Theseus out of the Cretan labyrinth, but here, since Cibber is the center of the maze, there is no way out. He has become the spirit of the labyrinth, like Ovid's "monstrum biforme." The disorientation is radical.

The vision of Dulness's empire restored at the end of Book 3 is exciting enough to arouse Cibber briefly. The Book concludes with the only words he speaks in the entire episode: "Enough! Enough!" The "raptur'd Monarch" then ascends through the ivory gate of illusion, like Aeneas, and returns to the world. Might not this situation be seen as a parody of Adam's rapture at the prospect of the Redemption?

So spake th'Arch-Angel *Michaël*, then paus'd,
As at the World's great period; and our Sire
Replete with joy and wonder thus repli'd.

    O goodness infinite, goodness immense!
That all this good of evil shall produce,
And evil turn to good; more wonderful
Than that which by creation first brought forth
Light out of darkness! Full of doubt I stand,
Whether I should repent me now of sin
By mee done and occasion'd, or rejoice
Much more, that much more good thereof shall spring,
To God more glory, more good will to Men
From God, and over wrath grace shall abound.

                      (12.466-78)

Adam's joy at the Redemption is perhaps being mimicked in Cibber's ecstatic reaction to the prospect of the restoration of the kingdom of Dulness, and Pope also seems to have in mind an inversion of the *felix culpa*, the heart of Milton's providential scheme through which God converts evil into good. To Dulness and her devotees Pope's archpedant, Bentley, ascribes a corresponding function of the "uncreating Word" to turn good into evil. He boasts himself as

Thy mighty Scholiast, whose unweary'd pains
Made Horace dull, and humbled Milton's strains.
Turn what they will to Verse, their toil is vain,
Critics like me shall make it prose again.

                      (4.211-13)

For the creative power of the *Word*—Christ, as the *Logos* in the Gospel of St. John, as well as the literary imagination—Bentley substitutes the stultifying power of *words*:

Then thus: "Since Man from beast by Words is known,
Words are Man's province, Words we teach alone.

When Reason doubtful, like the Samian letter,
Points him two ways, the narrower is the better.
Plac'd at the door of Learning, youth to guide,
We never suffer it to stand too wide.
To ask, to guess, to know, as they commence,
As Fancy opens the quick springs of Sense,
We ply the Memory, we load the brain,
Bind rebel Wit, and double chain on chain,
Confine the thought, to exercise the breath;
And keep them in the pale of Words till death."

(4.149-60)

The metamorphoses worked by Dulness exhaust the symbolic and spiritual powers of language and reify it. In the course of the poem mind and meaning accumulate weight and density of a quasi-physical nature, which increasingly subjects them to the downward pull of gravity. (Pope is continually suggesting that civilization depends on aspiration and inspiration, which the Dunces, as shown above, reduce to "breath" [4.159].) This reductive process makes the influence of Dulness and the responses of her "sons" a simple illustration of Newton's first Law:

And now had Fame's posterior trumpet blown,
And all the Nations summon'd to the Throne.
The young, the old, who feel her inward sway,
One instinct seizes and transports away.
None need a guide, by sure Attraction led,
And strong impulsive gravity of Head:
None want a place, for all their Centre found,
Hung to the Goddess, and coher'd around.
Not closer, orb in orb, conglob'd are seen
The buzzing Bees about their dusky Queen.

The gath'ring number, as it moves along,
Involves a vast involuntary throng,
Who gently drawn, and struggling less and less,
Roll in her Vortex, and her pow'r confess.

(4.71-84)

The massive and compact involvement of the Dunces in the Vortex of Dulness is evoked in the slow, heavy, labyrinthine movement of sound and sense in such a line as "Involves a vast involuntary throng." As the mass of Dulness is increased by the "conglobing" of the Dunces around her, an "attractive power" that draws more and more into its orbit at an accelerating rate, one has an eerie anticipation of the phenomenon of the "black hole" that astronomers have recently discovered in outer space, and that results from the tremendous gravitational force exercised by a huge and dense mass of matter that can reduce its volume almost to the point of annihilation.[13]

The gravitational vortex, a fundamental and ubiquitous image of the power of Dulness, is not limited by the law of the conservation of matter. It is imagined by Pope to have the power to annihilate, for Dulness is finally conceived of as somewhat like Rochester's "Nothing." The final implication of this image, then, is that of a self-destroying artifact:

Yet, yet, one moment, one dim Ray of Light
Indulge, dread Chaos, and eternal Night!
Of darkness visible so much be lent,
As half to shew, half veil the deep Intent.
Ye Pow'rs whose Mysteries restor'd I sing,
To whom Time bears me on his rapid wing,
Suspend a while your force inertly strong,
Then take at once the Poet and the Song.

(4.1-8)

In other words, the reduction of spirit to matter leads finally to the annihilation of matter as it becomes involved in the downward-spinning vortex of Dulness.

The richest modern example of the labyrinth as motif can be traced in the wanderings of Joyce's Stephen Dedalus and Leopold Bloom. Joyce may well be the first writer since Virgil and Ovid to employ the Minoan myth in its full cycle and with the greatest possible range of allusions. In a recent article Diane Fortuna has brilliantly demonstrated the central importance of the labyrinth both as symbol and as structural principle in *A Portrait of the Artist as a Young Man*.[14] In brief, she has discovered that the first ten of the nineteen sections of *A Portrait* recount a labyrinthine downward movement in Stephen's career that reaches its nadir in the central and tenth episode:

> As he walked home with silent companions, a thick fog seemed to compass his mind. He waited in stupor of mind till it should lift and reveal what it had hidden. He ate his dinner with surly appetite, and when the meal was over and the greasestrewn plates lay abandoned on the table, he rose and went to the window, clearing the thick scum from his mouth with his tongue and licking it from his lips. So he has sunk to the state of a beast that licks his chaps after meat. This was the end; and a faint glimmer of fear began to pierce the fog of his mind. He pressed his face against the pane of the window and gazed out into the darkening street. Forms passed this way and that through the dull light, and that was life. The letters of the name of Dublin lay heavily upon his mind, pushing one another surlily hither and thither with slow boorish insistence. His soul was fattening, congealing into gross grease, plunging ever deeper in its dull fear into a sombre threatening dusk, while the body that was his stood, listless and dishonored, gazing out of darkened eyes, helpless, perturbed and human, for a bovine god to stare upon.[15]

In this abyss of despair and guilt Stephen suffers the darkness and disorientation that characterize experience at the center of the labyrinth or at the bottom of the vortex in Virgil, Ovid, Dante, and Pope.

But contrary to Stephen's own interpretations of his spiritual condition, Joyce shows that his fall is a precondition to his increasing freedom, as appears in subsequent episodes.

Stephen's imaginary encounter with a bovine god at the bottom
and center of a spiral labyrinth (a central motif in Minoan
art) must be regarded in some sense as a liberating initiation.
As Fortuna observes:

> Stephen's psychological development thereafter becomes
> more free. Having reached the center, he reverses his course
> to move out of the labyrinth. As he winds his way out, his
> mind is gradually released from its burden of sin; he rejects
> the priesthood in favor of art; and he is ready at the end of
> the novel to escape the beauty maze, as he calls it, and fly
> beyond the nets of nationality, language, and religion. He
> circles then ever outwards through more complex and mature
> levels until he finds, in aesthetics, the thread that carries
> him back out of the labyrinth.[16]

By implication, Stephen's "fall," which seemed to him bestial,
his descent into a labyrinth of disorientation, darkness, terror,
and despair, and his finding at the center of the labyrinth a
bovine god staring upon him, is clearly patterned after Theseus's
quest for and slaying of the Minotaur. Joyce, then, is suggesting
that the sensuality Stephen condemns in himself has perhaps
brought him closer to a recognition of the human condition.
At any rate, his descent into sin seems to have a purgative
function, for he eventually manages to escape, however
temporarily, from the labyrinth of his egotism. Richard Ellmann speaks of "Stephen's insistence that man must fall because (as he said in a *Portrait*) only through error (a word he
substitutes for sin(can one become fully human and achieve
liberation in life or art."[17] One might add that a clear reason
for Joyce's use of *error* rather than *sin* is to keep alive the
labyrinthine associations of what Virgil called the *inextricabilis
error* of the Daedalian maze. After he has rejected the priest-
hood and committed himself to knowledge as "the releasing
agent,"[18] rather than innocence, Stephen sees a beautiful girl

"with bare legs delicate as a crane's wading along the shore. She somehow embodies this newly won confidence in his power to live and create, and stirs him to exaltation:

> Her image had passed into his soul for ever and no word had broken the holy silence of his ecstasy. Her eyes had called him and his soul had leaped at the call. To live, to err, to fall, to triumph, to recreate life out of life! A wild angel had appeared to him, the angel of mortal youth and beauty, an envoy from the fair courts of life, to throw open before him in an instant of ecstasy the gates of all the ways of error and glory. (P. 172)

Although this passage may be somewhat vague in its rapture, it clearly establishes a link in Stephen's mind between "error" and creation. Furthermore, as Fortuna has revealed, behind Stephen's rapture at the lovely girl with cranelike legs is a reminiscence of Ariadne and the crane dance that the young men and maidens of Crete performed in celebration of her flight with Theseus from the Daedalian maze.[19] With this turn of the upward spiral, Stephen's liberation is almost completed, and the birdlike girl becomes the inspiration for his own flight at the end of the novel. The flight is not, of course, an unequivocal triumph, overshadowed as it is by Stephen's ambiguous identity as both Daedalus and Icarus. Joyce's brilliant adaptation of the myth of the Daedalian labyrinth is fundamentally faithful to the intricacies of irony and paradox in earlier versions of the the Minoan archetype.

Of course, the disposition of the nineteen parts of *A Portrait of the Artist as a Young Man* almost inevitably invites the curious reader of *Ulysses* to explore the celebrated tenth chapter ("The Wandering Rocks") for corresponding structural and thematic elements. Chapter 10, placed as it is in the middle of the book's eighteen chapters, and which itself contains nineteen sections, weaves upon the warp of Father Conmee's visit to Artane (chiefly reported in the first section) and the woof of the Viceroy's visit to the Mirus Bazaar at Balsbridge (reported in the last section), a labyrinthine web of coordinated and synchronic movements in which virtually all the characters, major and minor, appear at some point in the course of the hour—from three to four P.M.—allotted to it.

Having established the characters, problems, and perspectives of Stephen and Bloom in the first nine chapters, Joyce takes a long view of them in a fully articulated account of Dublin life during an hour in the afternoon of June 16, 1904. The centripetal and egocentric movement of the *Telemachia* (chapters 1-3, focused on Stephen) and the Odyssean adventures of Bloom (chapters 4-9) have brought the action of *Ulysses* to a point corresponding to the sojourn of Odysseus in Phaiacia. Up to chapter 10, all is preparation, expostion, and recapitulation, just as it is in the first half of the *Odyssey* (Books 1-12).

In introducing the episode of the Wandering Rocks as the armature of chapter 10, Joyce substituted in his schema an episode that, of course, never occurred in the *Odyssey*. Odysseus, warned by Circe, chose to avoid the Symplegades, whose clashing rocks no ship could survive, in favor of the limited risk of Scylla and Charybdis, which is the basis, of course, of chapter 9 in *Ulysses*, the scene in the National Library. There Stephen and Bloom both undergo ordeals— Stephen in attempting to present his *summa aesthetica* to an unsympathetic audience, Bloom in escaping from the mortifying sight of Molly's lover and in pursuit of material for the advertisement he is trying to prepare. In modifying the Homeric Scylla and Charybdis episode, Joyce involves both his heroes in the ordeal. For Stephen the problem is to steer between the simplistic epistemological views of his auditors. Some critics suggest he had to find his way between Platonism and Aristotelianism, between too ghostly a view of paternity and creativity (represented by John Eglinton and A.E.) and the reductively material view caricatured in Buck Mulligan's obscenities. For Stephen the opposing risks are also represented by the Roman and the British institutions, the Church and the State, which he finds oppressive. For him the ordeal ends in an uneasy and unresolved truce. On the steps of the Library, where once (in *A Portrait*) he saw birds of happy augury, there are now no birds at all. For him the ordeal ends on a note of passivity, with an appropriately Shakespearean echo from *Cymbeline*:

> Kind air defined the coigns of houses in Kildare Street,
> No birds. Frail from the housetops two plumes of smoke
> ascended, pluming, and in a flaw of softness softly were
> blown.
> Cease to strive. Peace of the druid priests of
> Cymbeline, hierophantic: from wide earth an altar.
> *Laud we the gods*
> *And let our crooked smokes climb to their nostrils*
> *From our bless'd altars.*[20]

Bloom's escape between Scylla and Charybdis takes the form of an apologetic passage out of the Library between Stephen and Buck Mulligan, perhaps suggesting an avoidance both of Mulligan's spiritual sterility and Stephen's fatherless despair. In any event, both for him and for Stephen the episode is a richly symbolic but indecisive experience.

Indeed, indecision is the keynote to chapter 10. Or, perhaps, incompleteness. The main movements of the chapter traced by Father Conmee and the Viceroy in their missions to the north and south of Dublin are not completed, and the activities of a large cast of minor characters are equally frustrated, tentative, trivial, or incomplete. Corny Kelleher reflectively spins a coffinlid. A one-legged sailor receives a penny thrown by Molly. One of the Daedalus girls tries to get money

for food from her father. Blazes Boylan flirts with the girl
in the fruit shop. Almidano Artifoni gives the unheeding
Stephen advice. Boylan's secretary idles at work. Stephen is
moved by his sister's misery but does nothing about it. And
so it goes. The really significant movement in the chapter is that
of a crumpled handbill proclaiming that "Elijah is coming!,"
which Bloom had dropped earlier from the O'Connell Bridge.
At one point the tide takes it east; at another, a flood tide
takes it west; then it is mentioned a third time as it is
passing eastward again, out of the Liffey toward Dublin Bay.
As Ellmann observes, "the dominant mood from the *Wandering
Rocks* through *Circe* is skepticism."[21] He goes on to say, of
"The Wandering Rocks":

> The world, as Emerson in another context announced, "lies
> broken and in heaps," in eighteen little heaps and a coda,
> to be precise; the number of this episode's parts duplicates
> the total number of episodes in *Ulysses*, like a distorting
> mirror-image, to challenge the book's order. Dublin asserts
> itself as micropolis, with petty debts, petty spies, petty
> rebellions, petty lives and deaths, as if to deny the artist's
> effort to make it into Bloomusalem. Against the insistent
> claim of significance in the first half of the book, insignificance
> offers itself as the true temper of life. Joyce said the episode
> was conceived as a "moving labyrinth between two banks" of
> the Liffey. The analogy was to the clashing and floating
> rocks in the Bosphorus, separating Asia from Europe,
> between which Jason's Argo had to sail. For this episode
> Joyce cavalierly neglected the *Odyssey*, where the adventure
> of the wandering rocks is avoided in favor of the Scylla-
> Charybdis adventure, and followed instead the *Argonautica*
> of Apollonius of Rhodes.[22]

Joyce may have been cavalier in neglecting the *Odyssey* for
this episode in favor of the *Argonautica*, but if the chapter
is considered in its Odyssean context, one can see that it

constitutes a nonevent and is thus in keeping with the mood of the chapter.

Leo Knuth, in a recent article, modifies Ellmann's view of the chapter as "eighteen little heaps and a coda." Knuth finds the episodes organized symmetrically around the tenth and central one, where Bloom buys Molly a book entitled *The Sweets of Sin*, with Father Conmee's peregrinations (episode 1) and the Viceroy's (episode 19) bracketing the rest of the chapter. Whether or not one goes along with his idea that the remaining episodes are also organized on the principle of bilateral symmetry, there can be little doubt that his main point, that chapter 10 has as its central episode and symbol a labyrinth that stands for "man's quest for the hidden center,"[23] is convincing. Under Merchant's Arch, Bloom stands at the center of the city of Dublin, which, "with the Royal and Grand Canals encircling it on its north and south sides, and with the Liffey bisecting it along its west-east axis, is virtually a circular labyrinth of streets."[24] Knuth has, of course, Joyce's authority for the labyrinthine style of the chapter, and he establishes with considerable ingenuity an abundance of evidence for putting Bloom at the center of the maze: episode 10 in chapter 10 is as close as one can get to the structural center of the book; the sorties of Father Conmee and the Viceroy as extended on the map describe an X, with Bloom virtually at its center; X as the Greek capital Chi (X) is an abbreviation for Christ, and Bloom is repeatedly associated with Christ symbols in this chapter, especially with the sheep and the fish. Moreover, in addition to the many references to crosses and crucifixion is Bloom's gift to Molly, *The Sweets of Sin* — a sin offering that can be reduced to S.O.S. — Save Our Souls. While this summary by no means does justice to the generally judicious ingenuity of Knuth's analysis, it does suggest the rich and pervasive symbolism that may be found throughout "The Wandering Rocks."

It may seem impossible to reconcile the view of chapter 10 as "eighteen little heaps and a coda" with Knuth's view that in it Joyce,

> forcing his reader's fancies to roam in the quaint mazes of his daedal art. . . , seems to invite comparison with Satan's "I will" (Isaiah 14:13-14), which marked the introduction of the sweets of sin into the universe — the Minotaur at the center of the labyrinth that prompts man to say: *Voglio, si opus sit* (SOS). And *sos* is Irish for peace.[25]

Knuth, however, shows the way from a view of "The Wandering Rocks" as a trivial and fond record of an hour in the life of a micropolis to a vision of the mythical potentialities that underlie this record. In "Joyce, Jung, and *Ulysses*" William P. Fitzpatrick[26] makes the point that "the world of *Ulysses* remains in cipher and in large measure closed to the consciousness of Stephen, Bloom, and Molly, but for us it becomes a 'living Cosmos, articulated and meaningful' when we decipher the symbols and know the myths."[27] He cites Mircea Eliade's definition:

> The man of societies in which myth is a living thing lives in a World that, though in cipher and mysterious, is open. "The World speaks" to man, and to understand its language he needs only to know the myths and decipher the symbols. The world is no longer an opaque mass of objects arbitrarily thrown together, it is a living cosmos, articulated and meaningful. In the last analysis *the World reveals itself as language*. It speaks to man through its own mode of being, through its structures and its rhythms.[28]

Perhaps the most ancient schism dividing Joyce's critics is that which sets in opposition the realists and the symbolists. I would suggest that insofar as chapter 10 of *Ulysses* is concerned, this is a nonissue, just as it is, I believe, for the book as a whole, which weds the low mimetic mode of realism to the profound and soaring potentialities of ancient Minoan myth. One of the most important aspects of Joyce's adaptation of the *Odyssey* as archetype for *Ulysses* is that the *Odyssey* showed the way for a kind of epic mélange in which *sublimitas* and *humilitas* could coexist; in which Odysseus, the "allround" (*polutropos*) Noman in search of home, could be an authentic model for Joyce's middle-class hero. To see only the low, realistic aspects, or to ignore them in favor of a mythical or symbolic schema, is to risk incurring the myopia of Bloom's most formidable opponent, the Citizen in "Cyclops."

Thus, while the activity in "The Wandering Rocks" or in *Ulysses* as a whole may be trivial on the realistic level, the Daedalian and Odyssean myths make it possible to see that, even in this humdrum city, there is a real capacity for heroic self-knowledge and self-fulfillment. This can only occur, according to Fitzpatrick, through a ritual rebirth, which, in terms of either protagonist's experience in *Ulysses*, is left merely potential and indeterminate. If Erasmus is "the king of but,"[29] Joyce may be the king of "perhaps." Stephen and Bloom develop, but the narrative does not by any means bring them to the recognitions and fulfillments that conclude the *Odyssey*. As Fitzpatrick puts it,

> Throughout *Ulysses*, Stephen develops by his conquest of repressive maternal figures. But this development occurs symbolically rather than actually. All during Bloomsday, Stephen is in a state of crisis, in a pivotal moment of becoming. His experience conditions him psychically for the future by extirpating his subjective attachment to the past. At the novel's conclusion Stephen is still a potential artist, yet through Joyce's exploitation of myth, imminently capable of realization.[30]

In the central episode of chapter 10, perhaps even at the

conclusion of the novel, Bloom is still only a potential father, a potential husband. Yet, in the labyrinthine center of *Ulysses*, "though unaware either of his role as an avatar of the mighty dead, Greek and Semite, or of his symbolic function at the center of the labyrinth, Bloom's search guides him to *Sweets of Sin*"—a title in which Knuth finds that the Hebrew sense of sin and the Greek sense of beauty are synthesized.[31]

One detail not mentioned by Knuth provides, in my opinion, a bit of conclusive evidence in support of his basic interpretation of "The Wandering Rocks." As Bloom leafs through *The Sweets of Sin* in the tenth episode, he is overwhelmed by erotic fantasies of "opulent curves," "heaving embonpoints," and "perfect lips." The reader is then told that "Warmth showered gently over him, cowing his flesh. Flesh yielded amid rumpled clothes. Whites of eyes swooning up. His nostrils arched themselves for prey" (p. 236). Just as Stephen, in the central episode of *A Portrait*, finds a bovine god at the heart of the labyrinth, so Bloom, in the central episode of *Ulysses*, finds a bovine goddess. It is entirely in keeping with Bloom's precarious masculinity that he should be *cowed*: that is part of the masochism that he finally gets rid of in the "Circe" episode. Yet it is also appropriate to his potentially more affirmative self that Bloom in fantasy should identify himself, however tenuously, with the aggressive male lover, perhaps the Bull God Zeus who got Minos on Europa (associated, of course, with the Bosphorus—Joyce's Liffey—a motif central to chapter 10). Furthermore, Bloom's ambiguous experience of dread and desire as he encounters the *mysterium tremendum* perfectly accords with Rudolf Otto's classic definition of it:

These two qualities, the daunting and the fascinating, now combine in a strange harmony of contrasts, and the resultant dual character of the numinous consciousness, to which the entire religious development bears witness, at any rate from the level of the "daemonic dread" onwards, is at once the strangest and the most noteworthy phenomenon in the whole history of religion. The daemonic-divine object may appear to the mind an object of horror and dread, but at the same time it is no less something that allures with a potent charm, and the creature who trembled before it, utterly *cowed* and cast down, has always at the same time the impulse to turn to it, nay even to make it somehow his own. "The mystery" is for him not merely something to be wondered at but something that entrances him; and beside that in it which bewilders and confounds, he feels a something that captivates and transports him with a strange ravishment, rising often enough to the pitch of dizzy intoxication; it is the Dionysiac-element in the numen.[32]

If one fastidiously dismisses *The Sweets of Sin* as simply a piece of debased subliterature, one misses its vital function as a possible clue leading out of the labyrinth, an instrument of metamorphosis (or metempsychosis) by which Bloom can regain his manhood and renew his relationship with Molly.

Thus Joyce employed the labyrinth to impart a fundamentally life-affirming character to his works, while implying that in order to be liberated, one must first be imprisoned; in order to be enlightened, one must first be darkened; in order to arise, one must first have descended. In using as epigraph for *A Portrait of the Artist as a Young Man* the words Ovid applies to Daedalus as he prepares for his flight from the island prison in Crete — *et ignotas animum dimittit in artes* (and now he turns his mind to arts unknown) — Joyce was indicating that for the liberation of his heroes and for his own liberation as an artist, the myth of the Minoan labyrinth was essential.

5

Conclusion

What happens when a new work of art is created is something
that happens simultaneously to all the works of art which
preceded it. The existing monuments form an ideal order
among themselves, which is modified by the introduction of
the new (the really new) work of art among them. The existing order is complete before the new work arrives; for order
to persist after the supervention of novelty, the *whole* existing
order must be, if ever so slightly, altered. . . .
— Eliot, "Tradition and the Individual Talent"

Eliot's seminal perception of the complexity with which
the individual talent "conforms" to the tradition is a text for
our times when the relation of poets to their great precursors is
so often seen through the anxieties and hostilities of the Oedipal
complex. Unquestionably, many poets have been overwhelmed
by the potency of their great forebears. Unquestionably, others
have undergone something like the painful experience of individuation described brilliantly by Edward Edinger, the Jungian

133

psychoanalyst, in his recent article, "The Tragic Hero: An Image of Individuation":

> Modern psychology can add another aspect to the significance of tragic drama. The tragic hero depicts the ego undergoing individuation. Individuation is, in part, a tragic process. We define it as the ego's progressive awareness of and relation to the Self. But, as Jung has taught us, "the experience of the self is always a defeat for the ego," and a defeat for the ego is experienced as tragedy.[1]

The process of individuation can be assisted by participation in athletic contests and also by attending the tragic theater of Dionysus. Edinger cites the following passage from *The Laws* of Plato:

> I say a man should be really serious about serious things, not about trifles; by nature it is *God* that deserves all our most zealous attention, while man, as already stated, has been created God's plaything—and that's the finest thing about him. So all of us, men and women, should spend our lives playing the best games—quite the reverse of what people think nowadays.[2]

For Plato *paidion*, play, can provide us with the opportunity to undergo the process of individuation without the catastrophic loss and suffering that often concludes the career of the tragic hero. Drama and other ritual arts can permit us to participate *vicariously* in the process, to experience the *agon* of the hero's contest with darkness or evil, the *pathos* of his suffering, the *threnos* or lamentation for the defeated hero.[3] But where the representative Greek tragedy usually ends with the *threnos*, Edinger, following Gilbert Murray, points to the fourth and final phase of the process, the *theophany*, "a rebirth of life on another level with a reversal of emotion from sorrow to joy."[4] A. C. Bradley, according to Edinger, "expresses beautifully how the fourth phase of the ritual drama of the year spirit, the phase of theophany, which no longer appears in the tragic drama itself, is transferred to the experience of the spectator."[5] Most of us are not Prince Hamlet, nor were meant to be, yet the experience of the tragedy may give us an opportunity for individuation that is ultimately not tragic, but a part of the divine comedy.

The process of individuation, whether tragic or comic, lies at the heart of Homeric epic. The archetypal Homeric tragic figures are Achilles and Hector. The archetypal comic figure in Homer is Odysseus. The whole drive of Homer's epics is to transcend the iron antinomies of tragic confrontations, like those of Achilles and Agamemnon, and to develop, through games, through art, through the myth of the dancing-floor of Ariadne and the courts of arbitration in the *hieros kuklos* of Achilles' shield, a myth and a culture of survival and reconciliation.

Two of our greatest modern artists, Milton and Joyce, divined this Homeric vision, and they added to and modified the epic tradition by assimilating and re-creating Homer. At the center of their heroic visions of man's fate we find Homer and especially the *Odyssey*. They help us to understand Homer; Homer helps us to understand them; and in the process we escape from the deadly single vision of Arnold's high seriousness to see that the most serious things are too serious to be treated seriously.

Even writers such as Pope and Waugh, who devote themselves chiefly to the satiric and mock-epic modes, implicitly represent, as in a lost-wax casting, the heroic vision of the divine comedy that is explicitly absent from their works. Great satire, as Dryden argued, is a form of the heroic.

Notes

Introduction

1. Louis I. Bredvold, "The Gloom of the Tory Satirists," in *Pope and His Contemporaries: Essays Presented to George Sherburn*, ed. James L. Clifford and Louis A. Landa (Oxford: Clarendon Press, 1949), pp. 1-19.

2. James Joyce, *Ulysses* (New York: Modern Library, 1961), pp. 327-28.

3. Northrop Frye, *Anatomy of Criticism: Four Essays* (Princeton, N.J.: Princeton University Press, 1957), p. 34.

4. Josef Pieper, *Leisure: The Basis of Culture*, trans. A. Dru (New York: New American Library, 1963).

5. Ibid., p. 45.

Chapter 1: Heroic Games

1. Johan Huizinga, *Homo Ludens: A Study of the Play Element in Culture* (Boston: The Beacon Press, 1955), p. 11.

2. 1 *Henry IV*, act 5, scene 4, lines 78-79. All subsequent references in text to Shakespeare's plays are to act, scene, and line (e.g., 5.4.78-79).

3. E. R. Dodds, *The Greeks and the Irrational* (Berkeley, Calif.: University of California Press, 1951).

4. Huizinga, *Homo Ludens*, pp. 76-77.

5. Michael Putnam, *The Poetry of the "Aeneid": Four Studies in Imaginative Unity and Design* (Cambridge, Mass.: Harvard University Press, 1965), p. 81.

6. Ibid.

7. Roger Caillois, *Les Jeux et les Hommes* (Paris: Gallimard, 1958), pp. 42-43.

8. Ibid., p. 101.

9. Emrys Jones, "Pope and Dulness," *Proceedings of the British Academy* 54 (1968):253.

10. Rudolf Ekstein, "Pleasure and Reality, Play and Work, Thought and Action—

Variations Of and On a Theme," *The Journal of Humanistic Psychology* 3 (1963):24.
11. Stanley Fish, "Standing Only: Christian Heroism in *Paradise Lost*," *Critical Quarterly* 9(1967):162-78.

Chapter 2: Gods at War

1. C. M. Bowra, *Tradition and Design in the "Iliad"* (Oxford: Clarendon Press, 1930), p. 239.
2. W. K, Wimsatt, Jr., *"Belinda Ludens:* Strife and Play in *The Rape of the Lock*," *New Literary History* 4(1972-73):357-74.
3. Samuel Johnson, *The Lives of the English Poets*, ed. G. B. Hill, 3 vols. (Oxford: Clarendon Press, 1905), 1:185.
4. Arnold Stein, "The War in Heaven," in *Answerable Style: Essays on "Paradise Lost"* (Minneapolis, Minn.: The University of Minnesota Press, 1953), pp. 17-37; Merritt Y. Hughes, "Milton's Celestial Battle and the Theogonies," in *Studies in Honor of T. W. Baldwin*, ed. D. C. Allen (Urbana, Ill.: University of Illinois Press, 1958), pp. 237-53; Joseph Summers, *The Muse's Method: An Introduction to "Paradise Lost"* (New York: W. W. Norton & Co., 1962), pp. 112-38; Stella Revard, "Milton's Critique of Heroic Warfare in *Paradise Lost* V and VI," *Studies in English Literature* 7(1967):119-39.
5. Joseph Addison, *The Spectator*, ed. Donald F. Bond, 5 vols. (Oxford: Clarendon Press, 1965), 3:232.
6. M. Conrad Hyers, "The Comic Profanation of the Sacred," in *Holy Laughter: Essays on Religion in the Comic Perspective*, ed. Hyers (New York: The Seabury Press, 1969), pp. 9-27.
7. "Milton has followed some of the heroic assumptions to their ultimate conclusions: what *if* two heroic forces, equal in numbers *and* in strength, did meet. If one were "impaired," the other would have some advantage, but neither could finally "win;" neither could achieve the unconditional surrender of the other. The alternate possibilities are, for human warriors, mutual destruction and death; for angelic ones, 'in perpetual fight they need must last/Endless and no solution will be found.' The analogy holds too, I believe, for the spiritual warfare without divine intervention. Human and angelic wars are absurd if one expects them really to resolve uncertain issues" (Summers, *The Muse's Method*, p. 152).

Chapter 3: Feast of Fools

1. Mircea Eliade, *Cosmos and History: The Myth of the Eternal Return*, trans. Willard R. Trask (New York: Harper & Row, 1959), p. 34.
2. Hugo Rahner, *Man at Play*, trans. B. Battershaw and E. Quinn (New York: Herder & Herder, 1967), p. 85.
3. Ibid., p. 3.
4. Ernst Kris, *Psychoanalytic Explorations in Art* (New York: Schocken Books, 1952), p. 180.
5. *Eutrapelia*, among the virtues mentioned in the *Nicomachean Ethics*, is a central concept in Rahner's *Man at Play*. The essence of his discussion, "Eutrapelia: A

Forgotten Virtue," appears in Hyers's *Holy Laughter.*

6. Kris, *Psychoanalytic Explorations in Art*, p. 180.

7. C. L. Barber, *Shakespeare's Festive Comedy* (Princeton, N.J.: Princeton University Press, 1959), p. 196.

8. Walter Kaiser, *Praisers of Folly: Erasmus, Rabelais, Shakespeare* (Cambridge, Mass.: Harvard University Press, 1966), p. 217.

9. Barber, *Shakespeare's Festive Comedy*, p. 219.

10. Ibid., p. 219.

11. Josef Pieper, *Leisure: The Basis of Culture*, trans. A. Dru (New York: New American Library, 1963), p. 45.

12. W. B. Stanford, ed., *The Odyssey of Homer*, 2 vols. (London: MacMillan & Co., 1950), 1:338-39.

13. M. Conrad Hyers, "The Comic Profanation of the Sacred," in *Holy Laughter: Essays on Religion in the Comic Perspective*, ed. Hyers (New York: The Seabury Press, 1969), p. 24.

14. "The fool that was Falstaff, ever a hard man to put down, even manages unexpectedly to have a final reincarnation in the tragic figure of Antony. Despite all their differences, Antony remains a kind of Falstaffian fool: he is given to wine and lust; he prefers the night of pleasure to the day of duty; he lives out of all order, out of all compass, he lacks the appropriate gravity of his years and is accused of dotage; he is a truant to honor and an enemy to the world and its wisdom" (Kaiser, *Praisers of Folly*, p. 277).

15. Rahner, *Man at Play*, p. 3.

16. Janet Adelman, *The Common Liar: An Essay on "Antony and Cleopatra"* (New Haven and London: Yale University Press, 1973), p. 163.

17. Blake to Thomas Butts, November 22, 1802, in Blake, *Complete Writings*, ed. Geoffrey Keynes (London, New York, Toronto: Oxford University Press, 1966), p. 818.

18. Adelman, *The Common Liar*, p. 124.

19. Ibid., p. 69.

20. Rosalie L. Colie, "Problems of Paradoxes," in Colie, *Paradoxia Epidemica: The Renaissance Tradition of Paradox* (Princeton, N.J.: Princeton University Press, 1966), pp. 15-23. Reprinted in Kathleen Williams, ed., *Twentieth Century Interpretations of "The Praise of Folly"* (Englewood Cliffs, N.J.: Prentice-Hall, 1969), pp. 92-97.

21. Clarence H. Miller, ed., *The Praise of Folie by Sir Thomas Chaloner* (London, New York, Toronto: Oxford University Press, 1965), p. 37. Italics original.

22. Colie, *Paradoxia Epidemica*, p. 25.

23. Ibid., p. 19.

24. Richard Sylvester, "The Problem of Unity in *The Praise of Folly*," *English Literary Renaissance* 6(1976):125-39.

25. Colie, *Paradoxia Epidemica*, p. 20.

26. Chaloner's translation is so obscure here that I quote from that of John Wilson (1668), reprinted in 1958 by the University of Michigan Press, pp. 119-20.

27. Kaiser, *Praisers of Folly*, p. 36.

28. 2 Cor. 1.

Chapter 4: The Mazy Dance

1. Robert W. Cruttwell, *Virgil's Mind at Work: An Analysis of the Symbolism of the "Aeneid"* (Oxford: Basil Blackwell, 1947).

2. From Virgil, the *Aeneid*, with an English translation by H. R. Fairclough (Cambridge, Mass.: Harvard University Press; London: William Heinemann, Ltd., 1946):

> Daedalus, ut fama est, fugiens Minoïa regna,
> praepetibus pinnis ausus se credere caelo,
> insuetum per iter gelidas enavit ad Arctos
> Chalcidicaque levis tandem super adstitit arce.
> redditus his primum terris tibi, Phoebe, sacravit
> remigium alarum posuitque immania templa.
> in foribus letum Androgeo; tum pendere poenas
> Cecropidae iussi, miserum! septena quotannis
> corpora natorum; stat ductis sortibus urna.
> contra elata mari respondet Gnosia tellus:
> his crudelis amor tauri suppostaque furto
> Pasiphaë mixtumque genus prolesque biformis
> Minotaurus inest, Veneris monumenta nefandae;
> hic labor ille domus et inextricabilis error; .
> magnum reginae sed enim miseratus amorem
> Daedalus ipse dolos tecti ambagesque resolvit,
> caeca regens filo vestigia.
>
> (6.14-30)

From *The "Aeneid" of Virgil*, trans. Allen Mandelbaum (New York: Bantam, 1972), pp. 105-6:

> When Daedalus — for so the tale is told —
> fled Minos' kingdom on swift wings and dared
> to trust his body to the sky, he floated
> along strange ways, up toward the frozen North
> until he gently came to rest upon
> the mountaintop of Chalcis. Here he was
> returned to earth, and here he dedicated
> his oar-like wings to you, Apollo; here
> he built a splendid temple in your honor.
> Upon the gates he carved Androgeos' death,
> and then the men of Athens, made to pay
> each year with seven bodies of their sons;
> before them stands the urn, the lots are drawn.
> And facing this, he set another scene:
> the land of Crete, rising out of the sea;
> **the inhuman longing of Pasiphaë,**

the lust that made her mate the bull by craft;
her mongrel son, the two-formed Minotaur,
a monument to her polluted passion.
And here the inextricable labyrinth,
the house of toil, was carved; but Daedalus
took pity on the princess Ariadne's
deep love, and he himself helped disentangle
the wiles and mazes of the palace; with
a thread he guided Theseus' blinded footsteps.

3. W. F. Jackson Knight, *Cumaean Gates: A Reference of the Sixth "Aeneid" to the Initiation Pattern* (Oxford: Basil Blackwell, 1936). Reprinted in Knight, *Vergil: Epic And Anthropology* (New York: Barnes & Noble, 1967).

4. Jean Paris, *Joyce par lui-même* (Paris: Editions du Seuil, n.d.).

5. From Ovid, *Metamorphoses*, with an English translation by Frank Justus Miller (Cambridge, Mass.: Harvard University Press; London: William Heinemann, Ltd., 1971):

Vota Iovi Minos taurorum corpora centum
solvit, ut egressus ratibus Curetida terram
contigit, et spoliis decorata est regia fixis.
creverat obprobium generis, foedumque patebat
matris adulterium monstri novitate biformis;
destinat hunc Minos thalamo removere pudorem
multiplicique domo caecisque includere tectis.
Daedalus ingenio fabrae celeberrimus artis
ponit opus turbatque notas et lumina flexu
ducit in errorem variarum ambage viarum.
non secus ac liquidus Phrygiis Maeandrus in arvis
ludit et ambiguo lapsu refluitque fluitque
occurrensque sibi venturas aspicit undas
et nunc ad fontes, nunc ad mare versus apertum
incertas exercet aquas, ita Daedalus implet
innumeras errore vias vixque ipse reverti
ad limen potuit: tanta est fallacia tecti.

Quo postquam geminam tauri iuvenisque figuram
clausit, et Actaeo bis pastum sanguine monstrum
tertia sors annis domuit repetita novenis,
utque ope virginea nullis iterata priorum
ianua difficilis filo est inventa relecto,
protinus Aegides rapta Minoide Diam
vela dedit comitemque suam crudelis in illo
litore destituit. . . .

Daedalus interea Cretan longumque perosus
exilium tactusque loci natalis amore

clausus erat pelago. "terras licet" inquit "et undas
obstruat: et caelum certe patet; ibimus illac:
omnia possideat, non possidet aera Minos."
dixit et ignotas animum dimittit in artes
naturamque novat. nam ponit in ordine pennas
a minima coeptas, longam breviore sequenti,
ut clivo crevisse putes: sic rustica quondam
fistula disparibus paulatim surgit avenis;
tum lino medias et ceris alligat imas
atque ita conpositas parvo curvamine flectit,
ut veras imitetur aves. puer Icarus una
stabat et ignarus, sua se tractare pericla,
ore renidenti modo, quas vaga moverat aura,
captabat plumas, flavam modo pollice ceram
mollibat lusuque suo mirabile patris
impediebat opus. postquam manus ultima coepto
inposita est, geminas opifex libravit in alas
ipse suum corpus motaque pependit in aura;
instruit et natum "medio" que "ut limite curras,
Icare," ait "moneo, ne, si demissior ibis,
unda gravet pennas, si celsior, ignis adurat:
inter utrumque vola. . . .

                              et iam Iunonia laeva
parte Samos (fuerant Delosque Parosque relictae)
dextra Lebinthus erat fecundaque melle Calymne,
cum puer audaci coepit gaudere volatu
deseruitque ducem caelique cupidine tractus
altius egit iter. rapidi vicinia solis
mollit odoratas, pennarum vincula, ceras;
tabuerant cerae: nudos quatit ille lacertos,
remigioque carens non ullas percipit auras,
oraque caerulea patrium clamantia nomen
excipiuntur aqua, quae nomen traxit ab illo.
at pater infelix, nec iam pater, "Icare," dixit,
"Icare," dixit, "ubi es? qua te regione requiram?"
"Icare" dicebat: pennas aspexit in undis
devovitque suas artes corpusque sepulcro
condidit, et tellus a nomine dicta sepulti.

                                    (8.153-76, 183-206, 220-35)

From Ovid, *The Metamorphoses*, trans. Horace Gregory (New York: Viking Press, 1958), pp. 219-22:

    When Minos landed on the coast of Crete,

He bled a hundred bulls to mighty Jove,
And decked his palace with the spoils of war.
And yet strange gossip tainted all his honours:
Proof that his wife was mounted by a bull
Was clear enough to all who saw her son,
Half-beast, half-man, a sulky, heavy creature.
To hide this symbol of his wife's mismating
He planned to house the creature in a maze,
An arbour with blind walls beyond the palace;
He turned to Daedalus, an architect,
Who was well known for artful craft and wit,
To make a labyrinth that tricked the eye.
Quite as Meander flows through Phrygian pastures,
Twisting its streams to sea or fountainhead,
The dubious waters turning left or right,
So Daedalus designed his winding maze;
And as one entered it, only a wary mind
Could find an exit to the world again —
Such was the cleverness of that strange arbour.

Within this maze Minos concealed the beast,
And at two seasons placed nine years apart
He fed the creature on Athenian blood;
But when a third nine years had made their round,
The monster faced the season of his doom:
Where other heroes failed, the son of Aegeus,
Led by young Ariadne, walked the maze,
And, winding up the thread that guided him,
Raped Minos' daughter and sailed off with her
To leave her on the island shores of Dia.

. . . .

Weary of exile, hating Crete, his prison,
Old Daedalus grew homesick for his country
Far out of sight beyond his walls — the sea.
"Though Minos owns this island, rules the waves,
The skies are open: my direction's clear.
Though he commands all else on earth below
His tyranny does not control the air."
So Daedalus turned his mind to subtle craft,
An unknown art that seemed to outwit nature:
He placed a row of feathers in neat order,
Each longer than the one that came before it
Until the feathers traced an inclined plane
That cast a shadow like the ancient pipes

That shepherds played, each reed another step
Unequal to the next. With cord and wax
He fixed them smartly at one end and middle,
Then curved them till they looked like eagles' wings
And as he worked boy Icarus stood near him,
His brilliant face lit up by his father's skill.
He played at snatching feathers from the air
And sealing them with wax (nor did he know
How close to danger came his lightest touch);
And as the artist made his miracles
The artless boy was often in his way.
At last the wings were done and Daedalus
Slipped them across his shoulders for a test
And flapped them cautiously to keep his balance,
And for a moment glided into the air.
He taught his son the trick and said, "Remember
To fly midway, for if you dip too low
The waves will weight your wings with thick saltwater,
And if you fly too high the flames of heaven
Will burn them from your sides.

. . . .

They flew past Juno's Samos on the left
And over Delos and the isle of Paros,
And on the right lay Lebinthus, Calymne,
A place made famous for its wealth in honey.
By this time Icarus began to feel the joy
Of beating wings in air and steered his course
Beyond his father's lead: all the wide sky
Was there to tempt him as he steered toward heaven.
Meanwhile the heat of sun struck at his back
And where his wings were joined, sweet-smelling fluid
Ran hot that once was wax. His naked arms
Whirled into wind; his lips, still calling out
His father's name, were gulfed in the dark sea.
And the unlucky man, no longer father,
Cried, "Icarus, where are you, Icarus,
Where are you hiding, Icarus, from me?"
Then as he called again, his eyes discovered
The boy's torn wings washed on the climbing waves.
He damned his art, his wretched cleverness,
Rescued the body and placed it in a tomb,
And where it lies the land's called Icarus.

6. From Homer, *Iliadis*, ed. D. B. Monro and T. W. Allen (Oxford: Clarendon Press, 1920):

'Εν δὲ χορὸν ποίκιλλε περικλυτὸς ἀμφιγυήεις,　　　590
τῷ ἴκελον οἷόν ποτ' ἐνὶ Κνωσῷ εὐρείῃ
Δαίδαλος ἤσκησεν καλλιπλοκάμῳ Ἀριάδνῃ.
ἔνθα μὲν ἠίθεοι καὶ παρθένοι ἀλφεσίβοιαι
ὠρχεῦντ', ἀλλήλων ἐπὶ καρπῷ χεῖρας ἔχοντες.
τῶν δ' αἱ μὲν λεπτὰς ὀθόνας ἔχον, οἱ δὲ χιτῶνας　　595
εἴατ' ἐϋννήτους, ἦκα στίλβοντας ἐλαίῳ·
καί ῥ' αἱ μὲν καλὰς στεφάνας ἔχον, οἱ δὲ μαχαίρας
εἶχον χρυσείας ἐξ ἀργυρέων τελαμώνων.
οἱ δ' ὀτὲ μὲν θρέξασκον ἐπισταμένοισι πόδεσσι
ῥεῖα μάλ', ὡς ὅτε τις τροχὸν ἄρμενον ἐν παλάμῃσιν　　600
ἑζόμενος κεραμεὺς πειρήσεται, αἴ κε θέῃσιν·
ἄλλοτε δ' αὖ θρέξασκον ἐπὶ στίχας ἀλλήλοισι.
πολλὸς δ' ἱμερόεντα χορὸν περιίσταθ' ὅμιλος
τερπόμενοι· δοιὼ δὲ κυβιστητῆρε κατ' αὐτοὺς　　604, 605
μολπῆς ἐξάρχοντες ἐδίνευον κατὰ μέσσους.

From *The Iliad: Homer*, trans. Robert Fitzgerald (Garden City, N.Y.: Anchor Press/Doubleday, 1974), p. 454:

　　　　　　　A dancing floor as well
he fashioned, like that one in royal Knossos
Daidalos made for the Princess Ariadne.
Here young men and the most desired young girls
were dancing, linked, touching each other's wrists,
the girls in linen, in soft gowns, the men
in well-knit khitons given a gloss with oil;
the girls wore garlands, and the men had daggers
golden-hilted, hung on silver lanyards.
Trained and adept, they circled there with ease
the way a potter sitting at his wheel
will give it a practice twirl between his palms
to see it run: or else, again, in lines
as though in ranks, they moved on one another:
magical dancing! All around, a crowd
stood spellbound as two tumblers led the beat
with spins and handsprings through the company.

7. From Virgil, the *Aeneid*, with Eng. trans. by Fairclough:

　　At pater Aeneas nondum certamine misso
custodem ad sese comitemque impubis Iuli
Epityden vocat et fidam sic fatur ad aurem:

"vade age et Ascanio, si iam puerile paratum
agmen habet secum cursusque instruxit equorum,
ducat avo turmas et sese ostendat in armis,
dic," ait. ipse omnem longo decedere circo
infusum populum et campos iubet esse patentis.
incedunt pueri pariterque ante ora parentum
frenatis lucent in equis, quos omnis euntis
Trinacriae mirata fremit Troiaeque iuventus.
omnibus in morem tonsa coma pressa corona;
cornea bina ferunt praefixa hastilia ferro,
pars levis umero pharetras; it pectore summo
flexilis obtorti per collum circulus auri.
tres equitum numero turmae ternique vagantur
ductores; pueri bis seni quemque secuti
agmine partito fulgent paribusque magistris.
una acies iuvenum, ducit quam parvus ovantem
nomen avi referens Priamus, tua clara, Polite,
progenies, auctura Italos; quem Thracius albis
portat equus bicolor maculis, vestigia primi
alba pedis frontemque ostentans arduus albam.
alter Atys, genus unde Atii duxere Latini,
parvus Atys pueroque puer dilectus Iulo.
extremus formaque ante omnis pulcher Iulus
Sidonia est invectus equo, candida Dido
esse sui dederat monumentum et pignus amoris.
cetera Trinacriis pubes senioris Acestae
fertur equis.
excipiunt plausu pavidos gaudentque tuentes
Dardanidae veterumque adgnoscunt ora parentum.
postquam omnem laeti consessum oculosque suorum
lustravere in equis, signum clamore paratis
Epytides longe dedit insonuitque flagello.
olli discurrere pares atque agmina terni
diductis solvere choris rursusque vocati
convertere vias infestaque tela tulere.
inde alios ineunt cursus aliosque recursus
adversi spatiis, alternosque orbibus orbis
impediunt, pugnaeque cient simulacra sub armis;
et nunc terga fuga nudant, nunc spicula vertunt
infensi, facta pariter nunc pace feruntur.
ut quondam Creta fertur Labyrinthus in alta
parietibus textum caecis iter ancipitemque
mille viis habuisse dolum, qua signa sequendi
falleret indeprensus et inremeabilis error:

haud alio Teucrum nati vestigia cursu
impediunt texuntque fugas et proelia ludo,
delphinum similes, qui per maria umida nando
Carpathium Libycumque secant luduntque per undas.
hunc morem cursus atque haec certamina primus
Ascanius, Longam muris cum cingeret Albam,
rettulit et Priscos docuit celebrare Latinos,
quo puer ipse modo, secum quo Troia pubes;
Albani docuere suos; hinc maxima porro
accepit Roma et Patrium servavit honorem;
Troiaque nunc pueri, Troianum dicitur agmen.
hac celebrata tenus sancto certamina patri.

(5.545-603)

From The "Aeneid" of Virgil, trans. Mandelbaum, pp. 122-24:

But while the contest still was underway,
father Aeneas calls for Epytides,
the guardian and companion of young Iulus,
and whispers this into his trusted ear:
"Go now and tell Ascanius that if
his band of boys is ready with him, if
his horses are arrayed for the maneuvers,
then he can lead his squadrons out to honor
Anchises and can show himself in arms."
Then he himself calls for the crowding throng
to quit the long arena, clear the field.
The boys advance high on their bridled horses;
in even ranks, before their parents' eyes,
they glitter; as they pass, the men of Troy
and Sicily admiringly murmur.
And all, as custom calls for, have their hair
bound with a wreath of clipped leaves; and each bears
two cornel lances tipped with iron heads;
and some have polished quivers on their shoulders;
and high upon his chest, down from the neck,
each wears a pliant chain of twisted gold.
The squads are three in number, and three captains
parade, with twice-six boys behind each captain;
they gleam in ranks of six, each with a leader.
One band of boys is led by a triumphant
small Priam, who renews the name of his
grandfather—your bright son, Polites, destined
to swell the race of the Italians;
he rides upon a dappled Thracian stallion,

spotted with white, which as it paces, shows
white pasterns and a forehead high and white.
Next Atys rides, from whom the Atian
Latins have drawn their lineage — the little
Atys, a boy loved by the boy Iulus.
The last and handsomest of all, Iulus,
is mounted on a horse from Sidon, one
fair Dido gave him as memorial
and pledge of love. The other boys ride on
Sicilian horses from Acestes' stable.

The cheering Dardans greet the anxious squadrons
and watching those young faces, recognizing
the features of their ancestors, are glad.
And when the boys had crossed the whole enclosure,
had ridden happily before their elders,
then Epytides gave the signal shout
from far and cracked his whip. They rode apart,
to right and left, in equal ranks; the three
squadrons had split their columns into two
separate bands; and then, called back again,
they wheeled around and charged like enemies
with leveled lances. Now they start new marches
and countermarches in the space between them;
and interweaving circle into circle
in alternation, armed, they mime a battle.
And now they bare their backs in flight, and now,
peace made between them, gallop side by side.
As once, in ancient days, so it is said,
the labyrinth in high Crete had a path
built out of blind walls, an ambiguous
maze of a thousand ways, a winding course
that mocked all signs of finding a way out,
a puzzle that was irresolvable
and irretraceable: in such a course,
so intricate, the sons of Troy maneuver;
they interweave in sport of flight and battle
like dolphins which, when swimming liquid seas,
will cleave the Libyan and Carpathian deeps
and play among the waves. Ascanius
renewed, in later days, this way of riding,
these contests, when he girded Alba Longa
with walls and taught the early Latins how
to celebrate these games as he had done
beside the Trojan boys when he was young.

The Albans taught their sons, and after them
great Rome received these games and carried on
this same ancestral celebration; now
the boys are called "Troy" and their band, "the Trojans,"
Such were the competitions they observed
in honor of Aeneas' holy father.

8. "The primary idea of the labyrinthine form, which still demands great insistence, is the exclusion of hostile beings or influences. First this form is used in building, practically. Then it becomes more symbolic, but is supposed to be effective, even when it appears as a mere drawing on the ground, according to the theory of sympathetic magic. Even the lines of the drawing may be invisible. The very enactment by moving of a labyrinthine path may be expected to exercise a labyrinthine, exclusive effect. This is the meaning of a maze dance or other maze ritual. . . .The central evidence for this is an Etruscan vase and a passage of Vergil" (Knight, *Vergil: Epic and Anthropology*, p. 203).

9. "Le labyrinthe est double: si ses couloirs sinueux evoquent les tortures de la gehenne, ils conduisent aussi vers quelque lieu ou s'accomplira l'illumination" (Paris, *Joyce par lui-même*, p. 105).

10. Sir James G. Frazer relates the two to a common origin in *The Dying God* (London: MacMillan, 1911), pp. 75-76.

11. C. R. Deedes, "The Labyrinth," in *The Labyrinth: Further Studies in the Relation between Myth and Ritual in the Ancient World*, ed. S. H. Hooke (London: S.P.C.K., 1935), p. 42.

12. G. R. Levy, *The Gate of Horn: A Study of the Religious Conceptions of the Stone Age, and Their Influence upon European Thought* (London: Faber & Faber, 1948).

13. Walter Sullivan, "Curiouser and Curiouser: A Hole in the Sky," *New York Times Magazine*, July, 14, 1974.

14. Diane Fortuna, "The Labyrinth as Controlling Image in Joyce's *A Portrait of the Artist as a Young Man*," *Bulletin of the New York Public Library* 76(1972):120-80.

15. James Joyce, *A Portrait of the Artist as a Young Man* (New York: Viking, 1965), p. 111.

16. Fortuna, "The Labyrinth as Controlling Image," p. 141.

17. Richard Ellmann, *Ulysses on the Liffey* (New York: Oxford University Press, 1972), p. 93.

18. Ibid.

19. Cf. Frazer, *The Dying God*, p. 75: "Moreover, when Theseus landed with Ariadne in Delos on the Return from Crete, he and the young companions whom he had rescued from the Minotaur are said to have danced a mazy dance in imitation of the intricate windings of the labyrinth; on account of its sinuous turns the dance was called 'the Crane.' "

20. Joyce, *Ulysses*, p. 218. Italics original.

21. Ellman, *Ulysses on the Liffey*, p. 96.

22. Ibid., p. 91.

23. Leo Knuth, "A Bathymetric Reading of Joyce's *Ulysses*, Chapter X," *James Joyce Quarterly* 9 (1972):405-22.

24. Ibid., p. 406.

25. Ibid., pp. 418-19.

26. William P. Fitzpatrick, "Joyce, Jung, and *Ulysses*," *James Joyce Quarterly* 11 (1974):123-43.

27. Ibid., p. 125.

28. Mircea Eliade, *Myth and Reality*, trans. Willard R. Trask (New York: Harper and Row, 1963), p. 81. Italics original.

29. Kaiser, *Praisers of Folly*, p. 54.

30. Fitzpatrick, "Joyce, Jung, and 'Ulysses'," pp. 124-25.

31. Knuth, "A Bathymetric Reading of *Ulysses*, Chapter X," p. 418.

32. Rudolf Otto, *The Idea of the Holy: An Inquiry into the Non-Rational Factor in the Idea of the Divine and Its Relation to the Rational*, trans. John W. Harvey (London: Oxford University Press, 1950).

Chapter 5: Conclusion

1. Edward F. Edinger, "The Tragic Hero: An Image of Individuation," *Parabola: Myth and the Quest for Meaning* 1 (1976):68.

2. Plato *Laws* 7.803C.

3. Edinger, "The Tragic Hero," p. 68.

4. Ibid.

5. Ibid., p. 69.

Selected Bibliography

Primary Sources

Erasmus, Desiderius. *The Praise of Folie by Sir Thomas Chaloner.* by Clarence H. Miller. Early English Text Society Original Series 257. London, New York, Toronto: Oxford University Press, 1965.

Homer. *Iliadis.* Edited by D. B. Monro and T. W. Allen. Oxford: Clarendon Press, 1920.

———. *The Iliad.* Translated by Robert Fitzgerald. Garden City, N.Y.: Doubleday, 1974.

———. *The Odyssey.* Edited by W. B. Stanford. 2 vols. London: MacMillan & Co., 1950.

———. *The Odyssey.* Translated by Robert Fitzgerald. Garden City, N.Y.: Doubleday, 1961.

Joyce, James. *A Portrait of the Artist as a Young Man.* New York: Viking Press, 1964.

———. *Ulysses.* New York: Modern Library, 1961.

Milton, John. *Paradise Lost.* Edited by Merritt Y. Hughes. New York: The Odyssey Press, 1962.

Ovid. *Metamorphoses*. With an English translation by Frank Justus Miller. Cambridge, Mass.: Harvard University Press; London: William Heinemann, Ltd., 1971.

———. *The Metamorphoses*. Translated by Horace Gregory. New York: The Viking Press, 1958.

Pope, Alexander. *Poems*. Edited by John Butt. New Haven, Conn.: Yale University Press, 1963.

Shakespeare, William. *Antony and Cleopatra*. Edited by Barbara Everett. New York: The New American Library, 1964.

———. *Henry IV, Part One*. Edited by Maynard Mack. New York: The New American Library, 1965.

Virgil. *Aeneid*. With an English translation by H. R. Fairclough. Cambridge, Mass.: Harvard University Press; London: William Heinemann, Ltd., 1946.

———. *The "Aeneid" of Virgil*. Translated by Allen Mandelbaum. New York: Bantam, 1972.

Waugh, Evelyn. *A Handful of Dust* and *Decline and Fall*. New York: Dell Publishing Co., 1959.

Secondary Sources

Addison, Joseph. *The Spectator*. Edited by Donald F. Bond. 5 vols. Oxford: Clarendon Press, 1965.

Adelman, Janet. *The Common Liar: An Essay on "Antony and Cleopatra."* New Haven and London: Yale University Press, 1973.

Barber, C. L. *Shakespeare's Festive Comedy: A Study of Dramatic Form and its Relation to Social Custom*. Princeton, N.J.: Princeton University Press, 1959.

Becker, Ernest. *The Denial of Death*. New York: The Free Press, 1973.

Blake, William. *Complete Writings*. Edited by Geoffrey Keynes. London, New York, Toronto: Oxford University Press, 1966.

Bowra, C. M. *Tradition and Design in the "Iliad."* Oxford: Clarendon Press, 1930.

Bredvold, Louis I. "The Gloom of the Tory Satirists." In *Pope and his Contemporaries: Essays Presented to George Sherburn*, edited by James L. Clifford and Louis A. Landa. Oxford: Clarendon Press, 1949.

Caillois, Roger. *Les Jeux et les Hommes*. Paris: Gallimard, 1958.

Colie, Rosalie L. *Paradoxia Epidemica: The Renaissance Tradition of Paradox*. Princeton, N.J.: Princeton University Press, 1966.

Cruttwell, Robert W. *Virgil's Mind at Work: An Analysis of the Symbolism of the "Aeneid."* Oxford: Basil Blackwell, 1947.

Deedes, C. R. "The Labyrinth." In *The Labyrinth: Further Studies in the Relation between Myth and Ritual in the Ancient World*, edited by S. H. Hooke. London: The Society for the Promotion of Christian Knowledge, 1935.

Dodds, E. R. *The Greeks and the Irrational*. Berkeley, Calif.: University of California Press, 1951.

Edinger, Edward F. "The Tragic Hero: An Image of Individuation," *Parabola: Myth and the Quest for Meaning* 1 (1976): 59-69.

Ekstein, Rudolf. "Pleasure and Reality, Play and Work, Thought and Action—Variations Of and On a Theme." *The Journal of Humanistic Psychology* 3 (1963):20-31.

Eliade, Mircea. *Cosmos and History: The Myth of the Eternal Return*. Translated by Willard R. Trask. New York: Harper & Row, 1959.

———. *Myth and Reality*. Translated by Willard R. Trask. New York: Harper & Row, 1963.

Ellmann, Richard. *Ulysses on the Liffey*. New York: Oxford University Press, 1972.

Fish, Stanley. "Standing Only: Christian Heroism in *Paradise Lost*." *Critical Quarterly* 9 (1967):162-78.

Fitzpatrick, William P. "Joyce, Jung, and *Ulysses*." *James Joyce Quarterly* 11 (1974):123-43.

Fortuna, Diane. "The Labyrinth as Controlling Image in Joyce's *A Portrait of the Artist as a Young Man*." *Bulletin of the New York Public Library* 76 (1972):120-80.

Frazer, Sir James G. *The Dying God*. London: MacMillan, 1911.

Frye, Northrop. *Anatomy of Criticism: Four Essays*. Princeton, N.J.: Princeton University Press, 1957.

Hughes, Merritt Y. "Milton's Celestial Battle and the Theogonies." In *Studies in Honor of T. W. Baldwin*, edited by D. C. Allen. Urbana, Ill.: University of Illinois Press, 1958.

Huizinga, Johan. *Homo Ludens: A Study of the Play Element in Culture*. Boston: The Beacon Press, 1955.

Hyers, M. Conrad. "The Comic Profanation of the Sacred." In *Holy Laughter: Essays on Religion in the Comic Perspective*, edited by Hyers. New York: The Seabury Press, 1969.

Johnson, Samuel. *The Lives of the English Poets*. Edited by G. B. Hill. 3 vols. Oxford: Clarendon Press, 1905.

Jones, Emrys. "Pope and Dulness." *Proceedings of the British Academy* 54 (1968).

Kaiser, Walter. *Praisers of Folly: Erasmus, Rabelais, Shakespeare*. Cambridge, Mass.: Harvard University Press, 1963.

Knight, W. F. Jackson. *Cumaean Gates: A Reference of the Sixth "Aeneid" to the Initiation Pattern*. Oxford: Basil Blackwell, 1936. Reprinted in Knight's *Vergil: Epic and Anthropology*. New York: Barnes & Noble, 1967.

Knuth, Leo. "A Bathymetric Reading of Joyce's *Ulysses*, Chapter X." *James Joyce Quarterly* 9 (1972):405-22.

Kris, Ernst. *Psychoanalytic Explorations in Art*. New York: Schocken Books, 1952.

Levy, G. R. *The Gate of Horn: A Study of the Religious Conceptions of the Stone Age, and their Influence upon European Thought*. London: Faber & Faber, 1948.

Otto, Rudolf. *The Idea of the Holy: An Inquiry into the Non-Rational Factor in the Idea of the Divine and its Relation to the Rational*. Translated by John W. Harvey. London: Oxford University Press, 1950.

Paris, Jean. *Joyce par lui-même*. Paris: Editions du Seuil, n.d.

Pieper, Josef. *Leisure: The Basis of Culture*. Translated by A. Dru. New York: New American Library, 1963.

Putnam, Michael. *The Poetry of the "Aeneid": Four Studies in Imaginative Unity and Design*. Cambridge, Mass.: Harvard University Press, 1965.

Rahner, Hugo. *Man at Play*. Translated by B. Battershaw and E. Quinn. New York: Herder & Herder, 1967.

Revard, Stella. "Milton's Critique of Heroic Warfare in *Paradise Lost* V and VI." *Studies in English Literature* 7 (1967):119-39.

Stein, Arnold. *Answerable Style: Essays on "Paradise Lost."* Minneapolis, Minn.: The University of Minnesota Press, 1953.

Summers, Joseph. *The Muse's Method: An Introduction to "Paradise Lost."* New York: W. W. Norton & Co., 1962.

Sylvester, Richard S. "The Problem of Unity in *The Praise of Folly.*" *English Literary Renaissance* 6 (1976):125-39.

Wimsatt, William K., Jr. "Belinda Ludens: Strife and Play in *The Rape of the Lock.*" *New Literary History* 4 (1972-73):357-74.

Index

155